Using Microcomputers for Planning and Management Support

William L. Tetlow, *Editor*

NEW DIRECTIONS FOR INSTITUTIONAL RESEARCH
Sponsored by the Association for Institutional Research
MARVIN W. PETERSON, PATRICK T. TERENZINI
Editors-in-Chief

Number 44, December 1984

Paperback sourcebooks in
The Jossey-Bass Higher Education Series

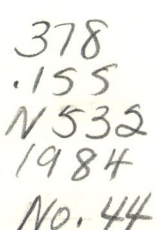

Jossey-Bass Inc., Publishers
San Francisco • Washington • London

William L. Tetlow (Ed.).
Using Microcomputers for Planning and Management Support.
New Directions for Institutional Research, no. 44.
Volume XI, number 4.
San Francisco: Jossey-Bass, 1984

New Directions for Institutional Research Series
Marvin W. Peterson, Patrick T. Terenzini, *Editors-in-Chief*

Copyright © 1984 by Jossey-Bass Inc., Publishers
and
Jossey-Bass Limited

Copyright under International, Pan American, and Universal Copyright Conventions. All rights reserved. No part of this issue may be reproduced in any form—except for brief quotation (not to exceed 500 words) in a review or professional work—without permission in writing from the publishers.

New Directions for Institutional Research (publication number USPS 098-830) is published quarterly by Jossey-Bass Inc., Publishers, and is sponsored by the Association for Institutional Research. The volume and issue numbers above are included for the convenience of libraries. Second-class postage rates paid at San Francisco, California, and at additional mailing offices.

Correspondence:
Subscriptions, single-issue orders, change of address notices, undelivered copies, and other correspondence should be sent to Subscriptions, Jossey-Bass Inc., Publishers, 433 California Street, San Francisco California 94104.

Editorial correspondence should be sent to the Editor-in-Chief, Marvin W. Peterson, Center for the Study of Higher Education, University of Michigan, Ann Arbor, Michigan 48109, or Patrick T. Terenzini, Office of Institutional Research, SUNY, Albany, New York 12222.

Library of Congress Catalogue Card Number LC 83-82730
International Standard Serial Number ISSN 0271-0579
International Standard Book Number ISBN 87589-777-0

Cover art by Willi Baum
Manufactured in the United States of America

Ordering Information

The paperback sourcebooks listed below are published quarterly and can be ordered either by subscription or single-copy.

Subscriptions cost $35.00 per year for institutions, agencies, and libraries. Individuals can subscribe at the special rate of $25.00 per year *if payment is by personal check.* (Note that the full rate of $35.00 applies if payment is by institutional check, even if the subscription is designated for an individual.) Standing orders are accepted. Subscriptions normally begin with the first of the four sourcebooks in the current publication year of the series. When ordering, please indicate if you prefer your subscription to begin with the first issue of the *coming* year.

Single copies are available at $8.95 when payment accompanies order, and *all single-copy orders under $25.00 must include payment.* (California, New Jersey, New York, and Washington, D.C., residents please include appropriate sales tax.) For billed orders, cost per copy is $8.95 plus postage and handling. (Prices subject to change without notice.)

Bulk orders (ten or more copies) of any individual sourcebook are available at the following discounted prices: 10-49 copies, $8.05 each; 50-100 copies, $7.15 each; over 100 copies, *inquire.* Sales tax and postage and handling charges apply as for single copy orders.

To ensure correct and prompt delivery, all orders must give either the *name of an individual* or an *official purchase order number.* Please submit your order as follows:

Subscriptions: specify series and year subscription is to begin.
Single Copies: specify sourcebook code (such as, IR8) and first two words of title.

Mail orders for United States and Possessions, Latin America, Canada, Japan, Australia, and New Zealand to:
Jossey-Bass Inc., Publishers
433 California Street
San Francisco, California 94104

Mail orders for all other parts of the world to:
Jossey-Bass Limited
28 Banner Street
London EC1Y 8QE

New Directions for Institutional Research Series
Marvin W. Peterson, Patrick T. Terenzini
Editors-in-Chief

IR1 *Evaluating Institutions for Accountability,* Howard R. Bowen
IR2 *Assessing Faculty Effort,* James I. Doi
IR3 *Toward Affirmative Action,* Lucy W. Sells
IR4 *Organizing Nontraditional Study,* Samuel Baskin

IR5 *Evaluating Statewide Boards,* Robert O. Berdahl
IR6 *Assuring Academic Progress Without Growth,* Allan M. Cartter
IR7 *Responding to Changing Human Resource Needs,* Paul Heist, Jonathan R. Warren
IR8 *Measuring and Increasing Academic Productivity,* Robert A. Wallhaus
IR9 *Assessing Computer-Based System Models,* Thomas R. Mason
IR10 *Examining Departmental Management,* James Smart, James Montgomery
IR11 *Allocating Resources Among Departments,* Paul L. Dressel, Lou Anna Kimsey Simon
IR12 *Benefiting from Interinstitutional Research,* Marvin W. Peterson
IR13 *Applying Analytic Methods to Planning and Management,* David S. P. Hopkins, Roger G. Schroeder
IR14 *Protecting Individual Rights to Privacy in Higher Education,* Alton L. Taylor
IR15 *Appraising Information Needs of Decision Makers,* Carl R. Adams
IR16 *Increasing the Public Accountability of Higher Education,* John K. Folger
IR17 *Analyzing and Constructing Cost,* Meredith A. Gonyea
IR18 *Employing Part-Time Faculty,* David W. Leslie
IR19 *Using Goals in Research and Planning,* Robert Fenske
IR20 *Evaluating Faculty Performance and Vitality,* Wayne C. Kirschling
IR21 *Developing a Total Marketing Plan,* John A. Lucas
IR22 *Examining New Trends in Administrative Computing,* E. Michael Staman
IR23 *Professional Development for Institutional Research,* Robert G. Cope
IR24 *Planning Rational Retrenchment,* Alfred L. Cooke
IR25 *The Impact of Student Financial Aid on Institutions,* Joe B. Henry
IR26 *The Autonomy of Public Colleges,* Paul L. Dressel
IR27 *Academic Program Evaluation,* Eugene C. Craven
IR28 *Academic Planning for the 1980s,* Richard B. Heydinger
IR29 *Institutional Assessment for Self-Improvement,* Richard I. Miller
IR30 *Coping with Faculty Reduction,* Stephen R. Hample
IR31 *Evaluation of Management and Planning Systems,* Nick L. Poulton
IR32 *Increasing the Use of Program Evaluation,* Jack Lindquist
IR33 *Effective Planned Change Strategies,* G. Melvin Hipps
IR34 *Qualitative Methods for Institutional Research,* Eileen Kuhns, S. V. Martorana
IR35 *Information Technology: Advances and Applications,* Bernard Sheehan
IR36 *Studying Student Attrition,* Ernest T. Pascarella
IR37 *Using Research for Strategic Planning,* Norman P. Uhl
IR38 *The Politics and Pragmatics of Institutional Research,* James W. Firnberg, William F. Lasher
IR39 *Applying Methods and Techniques of Futures Research,* James L. Morrison, William L. Renfro, Wayne I. Boucher
IR40 *College Faculty: Versatile Human Resources in a Period of Constraint,* Roger G. Baldwin, Robert T. Blackburn
IR41 *Determining the Effectiveness of Campus Services,* Robert A. Scott
IR42 *Issues in Pricing Undergraduate Education,* Larry H. Litten
IR43 *Responding to New Realities in Funding,* Larry L. Leslie

Contents

Editor's Notes 1
William L. Tetlow

Chapter 1. The Second Wave of Campus Computerization 5
William L. Tetlow
What higher education managers are experiencing is not a phenomenon unique to them but rather part of colliding waves of change that are a fundamental part of the era in which we live.

Chapter 2. The Changing Nature of Computer-Based Information Systems 11
Paul T. Brinkman
We are now entering a period in which the requirements of the end user are dominant, as computer-based information systems learn to speak the language of the manager.

Chapter 3. Using Microcomputers for Institutional Research 27
J. Lloyd Suttle
Many institutional researchers will find that the microcomputer leads to greater efficiency in everything that they do, especially in the two most critical elements of their jobs: thinking and communicating.

Chapter 4. Microware: Hard, Soft, and Firm 39
Leah R. Hutten
With more than 150 microcomputer manufacturers worldwide, a new vocabulary to untangle, and often contradictory and misleading advice from salespersons, there is a clear need to unravel the mysteries surrounding microcomputers.

Chapter 5. Using Microcomputers for Distributed Information Processing 53
Derek M. Jamieson, Kenneth H. MacKay
Microcomputers contribute to communications both in the direct sense by expediting word processing and other forms of electronic communication and in the indirect sense by facilitating communication and analysis among managers and researchers.

Chapter 6. Micros, Minis, and Mainframes 63
Vinod Chachra
For equivalent computer power, smaller computers are not more expensive than larger computers. The cost of computing in the immediate future will be governed not by hardware costs but rather by personnel, software, and communications costs.

Chapter 7. The Case for Decision Support Management 77
Paul Jedamus
The key to the success of decision support systems will be the way that institutional researchers integrate the wide variety of specific and personal systems into a viable and coordinated institutionwide system.

Chapter 8. A Jump Ahead... In Which Direction? 87
Mark Meredith
Before you embark in a new direction toward the new technology, several provocative questions concerning administrative acquisition and use of microcomputers deserve serious thought.

Chapter 9. Conclusion: Using Microcomputers for Planning and Management Support 93
William L. Tetlow
Microcomputer technology is direct, personal, and especially well suited for the task of decision support. Learning to use it constructively and effectively to improve higher education management is the challenge of the immediate future.

Index 99

The Association for Institutional Research was created in 1966 to benefit, assist, and advance research leading to improved understanding, planning, and operation of institutions of higher education. Publication policy is set by its Publications Board.

PUBLICATIONS BOARD
Stephen R. Hample (Chairperson), Montana State University
Ellen E. Chaffee, National Center for Higher Education Management Systems
Jean J. Endo, University of Colorado at Boulder
Cameron L. Fincher, University of Georgia
Richard B. Heydinger, University of Minnesota
Penny A. Wallhaus, Illinois Community College Board

EX-OFFICIO MEMBERS OF THE PUBLICATIONS BOARD
Charles F. Elton, University of Kentucky
Elizabeth F. Fox, University of Alabama in Birmingham
Gerald W. McLaughlin, Virginia Polytechnic Institute & State University
Marvin W. Peterson, University of Michigan
Patrick T. Terenzini, State University of New York at Albany

EDITORIAL ADVISORY BOARD
All members of the Publications Board and:
Frederick E. Balderston, University of California, Berkeley
Howard R. Bowen, Claremont Graduate School
Roberta D. Brown, Arkansas College
Lyman A. Glenny, University of California, Berkeley (retired)
David S. P. Hopkins, Stanford University
Roger G. Schroeder, University of Minnesota
Robert J. Silverman, Ohio State University
Martin A. Trow, University of California, Berkeley

For information about the Association for Institutional Research, write:

> AIR Executive Office
> 314 Stone Building
> Florida State University
> Tallahassee, FL 32306
>
> (904)644-4470

Editor's Notes

Just recently, I happened to open my Random House unabridged dictionary to the pages of words beginning with *micro-*. Since this dictionary had been my mainstay for several years, I was curious to see how it defined *microcomputer*. At first I was startled to see that the word was not listed. I then looked at the publishing date and found it to be 1966-1967. No wonder! Twenty years ago, I was plugging electrical wires called "patchcords" into sockets on a thing called a "breadboard" so that an electromechanical device could assist me in converting data to information. Now we live in a world where the supermarket clerk and the auto muffler installer are both using a microprocessor, laser optics, and nonvolatile magnetic bubble memories to provide us with service.

In his book, *The Micro Millenium* (1979), Christopher Evans convincingly asserts that a transformation of world society is taking place at all levels. He states that our future is being molded by a single, startling development in technology whose impact is just beginning to be felt. As did the Industrial Revolution, the "computer revolution will have an overwhelming and comprehensive impact, affecting every being on earth in every aspect of his or her life" (Evans, 1979, p. 5). I believe him—and so, I think, should you.

Recently, I was addressing financial executives from many colleges and universities on the subject of microcomputer trends. I used Alvin Toffler's (1981) concept of lifetimes as a means of easing the future shock and anxiety I knew some of them were feeling when it came to the subject of microcomputers. Toffler reduced mind-boggling numbers such as 50,000 years (man's estimated existence on Earth) to a useful size of 800 lifetimes by dividing the former by an average life span of sixty-two years. Then he points out that man lived in caves for the first 650 lifetimes, communicated via the printed word only in the last seven lifetimes, and used electricity only in this, the *present,* lifetime. No wonder my nearly twenty-year-old dictionary does not mention microcomputers! It does define both *computer* and *laser,* so maybe I can get another six months' use out of it before I trade it in for a new version.

I doubt that this sourcebook will be relevant for a whole lifetime; it may not even be as durable as my dictionary. Its purpose, however, is to try to provide a metaview of this chaotic, volatile, and rapidly changing computer revolution so that readers can be informed professionals and planners.

The microprocessor is the device that is accelerating the transformation of society. We need to know what it can and cannot do and how to integrate it

---

1-2-3 is a registered trademark of the Lotus Development Corporation. Super-Calc is a registered trademark of Sorcim, Inc. VisiCalc is a registered trademark of Software Arts, Inc. IFPS is a registered trademark of Execucom Systems Corporation.

effectively into both our professional and our personal lives. We need to select microcomputer components—hardware, firmware, and software—wisely so that we can make intelligent, creative, and appropriate applications of this useful tool. And, we in higher education need to heed John Naisbitt's (1982) advice to combine the high touch of personal responsibility with our high-tech tools so that we do not fall into the seductive trap of thinking that new tools are the solution.

Thus, in conceiving the contents of this sourcebook, I turned both to philosophers and to computer professionals. Paul T. Brinkman, a highly respected colleague of mine at the National Center for Higher Education Management Systems, is a philosopher who also acquired a Ph.D. in higher education finance. I asked him to sort out the conceptual gold nuggets from the rubble of buzzwords and acronyms. His training and devotion to epistemology, when brought to bear on this assignment, have led in Chapter Two to a concise and lucid primer on the evolution of information systems and the new developments spurred on by the advent of the microcomputer.

J. Lloyd Suttle, a former institutional research director at Yale University and now dean of administrative affairs at Yale College, was enlisted to describe and evaluate the applications of microcomputer technology to institutional research and planning tasks. There is no doubt that the practice of institutional research is, and will continue to be, affected profoundly by microtechnology. The clear and present danger is to misapply the technology or to overrate its usefulness. In Chapter Three, Suttle provides current professionals with useful and practical insights.

Whether you are convinced by media or salesperson hype, the thoughtful expositions of experts like Suttle, or by a desire not to be the last kid on the block to own one, you will soon acquire the ubiquitous microcomputer. When you do, you will find that Leah Hutten's advice in Chapter Four will help you to distinguish between RAMs and ROMs and enable you to select the necessary hardware and software that will enable you to harness the microcomputer's productive power.

In Chapter Five, Derek M. Jamieson and Kenneth H. MacKay, Canadian colleagues who manage to remain on the cutting edge of the effective application of technology to higher education management, portray in nontechnical language how the microcomputer can be used to communicate data, ideas, and information. They rely on their experience at Guelph University not only to map the options but also to provide critical insights about policy issues and potential traps for the unwary.

Vinod Chachra, a Vice-president at Virginia Polytechnic Institute and a leading expert and consultant on computers of all sizes and vintages, was asked to provide guidelines and suggestions for matching the appropriate type of computer to the appropriate task. His expertise is evident in Chapter Six, where he deals with major policy issues stemming from the application of computer technology to both academic and administrative problems.

While microcomputers can be used as key elements in building personal and specific decision support systems, the success of the venture lies in effective decision support management. Paul Jedamus, a professor of management science and information systems at the University of Colorado, states in Chapter Seven that the distributed computing revolution is not coming— because it is already here. But then, in the patois of a veteran Coloradan, he finds that most administrators in higher education are still living on beans and jackrabbits.

To end this sourcebook on a hard-hitting and realistic note and to further my aim of helping readers become informed users of microcomputers, I turned to another twenty-year veteran institutional research officer, Mark Meredith, who has a penchant for asking thoughtful and provocative questions. As we discussed the contents of Chapter Eight, I was reminded of a cartoon in which a mother kangaroo was giving advice to her young offspring. She sternly admonished, "It is no good being one jump ahead if you are headed in the wrong direction!" I wanted readers to be given some points to ponder. Meredith responded with several questions, each one posed in a positive spirit.

I believe that we owe a substantial debt to Steven Jobs, the inventor of the Apple microcomputer. He and the Apple unleashed the phenomenal creative talent that mankind possesses by giving to all of us a powerful and low-cost tool to exercise that creativity. Computers, once the preserve of an almost secret and monastic computer priesthood, are now more powerful, portable, and accessible than the ones I worked with at Cornell University twenty years ago.

Working on this sourcebook has been a labor of love, since I am a microcomputer enthusiast. In editing these chapters, I made extensive use of microcomputers. The authors used word processing software in preparing chapters. Half of the chapters were transmitted to me electronically, and I edited them on my own COMPAQ microcomputer. To complete the process, I left electronic mail messages on the authors' host computers wherever practical.

You, too, can make very effective use of microcomputers if you learn from these experts and follow their advice.

William L. Tetlow
Editor

References

Evans, C. *The Micro Millenium.* London: Viking, 1979.
Naisbitt, J. *Megatrends: Ten New Directions Transforming Our Lives.* New York: Warner, 1982.
Toffler, A. *The Third Wave.* New York: Bantam, 1981.

William L. Tetlow is director of computing resources and director of the Management Products Division at the National Center for Higher Education Management Systems (NCHEMS). He is past president of the Association for Institutional Research and for twenty years was a director of institutional research at universities in Canada and the United States.

The eclectic acquisition of microcomputers in higher education is not unique to it but rather part of colliding waves of change that are a fundamental part of the remarkable era in which we live.

The Second Wave of Campus Computerization

William L. Tetlow

College and university administrators are currently faced with a major dilemma concerning the acquisition, deployment, and effective use of microcomputer technology. While this low-cost and convenient technology is making major and innovative contributions to both academic and administrative aspects of higher education, it is often acquired and used in an eclectic fashion. "In many corporations, perhaps in yours, personal computers are springing up in the most surprising places, like mushrooms after the rain. They are inexpensive, and they can be used for a rich variety of applications—electronic spreadsheets, word processing, job scheduling, records management... the list is endless. Anyone with a little imagination can justify and, if necessary, bury the cost of a personal computer. Circumventing the corporations' traditional channels for authorizing the purchase of [computer] equipment has become a game played with increasing enthusiasm by those who have discovered the remarkable power of today's personal computer" (Stewart, 1983, p. 1).

The cumulative capital requirements for hardware, software, supplies, and training materials are staggering. Even the smallest institutions can anticipate a million-dollar need if attempts are made to satisfy the demands of faculty, students, and administrators. Many large institutions have already expended over a million dollars on microcomputer equipment, computer programs, furniture, and supplies, such as paper and carbon ribbons. This sum is in addition to the millions spent annually on hardware, software, supplies, and salaries for large campus mainframe computers and departmental research minicomputers.

Candid administrators will admit that they have an imprecise idea of the total funds expended, because the amounts involved in many of the purchases do not exceed the threshold value at which a review and approval procedure is invoked. Any faculty member who wished to avoid the delays and information requirements associated with the purchase of a $50,000 minicomputer could purchase twenty microcomputers, one at a time, from the supplies and expense line in the research, teaching, or administrative budget under his or her personal control. The subsequent ripple effect of purchases of software, supplies, maintenance, and so forth — to say nothing of the salary and wages involved — ultimately could place severe strains on the budget and major encumbrances on future budget options.

This massive acquisition of computer technology is having an effect on many campuses akin to that of a tidal wave hitting the coastline. Microcomputers are appearing everywhere, from scientific research labs to humanities classes and offices. Moreover, they come in over 150 basic varieties that are for the most part totally incompatible with one another. They are sapping productive time and energy as neophytes struggle with arcane terminology, incompatible combinations of equipment, and confusing, incomplete, and often erroneous instructions. A natural outgrowth of the confusion is the growing recognition and demand for training and standardization.

At the same time, however, microcomputers are liberating faculty, students, and staff alike as they are being applied in innovative and creative ways. For administrators, they offer solutions to chronic multiyear delays in the development of new application systems. They also offer direct, immediate, and personal analytic assistance that replaces and improves on previous procedures. Faculty members can do their own word processing and maintain personalized class notes in an efficient manner, which allows them to offer more individual attention to their students. Students use microcomputers for class assignments, term papers, and electronic messaging, and they have even created a new form of the dating game, romancing by computer.

Colliding Waves of Change

What higher education institutions are experiencing is not unique to them but rather part of colliding waves of change that are a fundamental part of the remarkable era in which we live. Alvin Toffler (1981, p. 5) uses the wave metaphor because "it helps us see beneath the raging surface of change." Christopher Evans (1979) went the extra step, labeling the current turmoil *the micro millenium*. Evans predicted that the changes in our lives brought about by the new technology would compare in significance and social upheaval with the changes that occurred in the Industrial Revolution.

Toffler (1981) sees our present society as a product of three great waves of changes. The first started nearly 10,000 years ago with the creation of an agricultural society. The second wave began 300 years ago with the onset of the Industrial Revolution, and it is now colliding with the third wave of pervasive technological change. According to Toffler, the guiding principles of the second wave of industrialization were standardization, synchronization, and specialization. Concentration of people and resources, sheer size, and centralization of power were also important hallmarks of this civilization. The third wave, while clashing and colliding with the second wave and causing tension and conflict in our personal and professional lives, is beginning to create a new culture, which synthesizes the technology of the future with the simpler values of the past. Technology has the liberating potential to decentralize, enhance our individuality, increase our options, and make us more human. For the most part, these changes are the direct result of a startling number of technological advances that have so subtly infiltrated our everyday lives that we rarely notice them.

Dominant Trends

Using the simple but powerful methodology of content analysis, which ascribes value to the space devoted in the press to news, John Naisbitt (1982) has concluded that there are several trends of change. He lists ten trends that are transforming and shaping our lives. In Naisbitt's opinion (1982, p. 9), "trends, like horses, are easier to ride in the direction they are already going."

While all these trends Naisbitt identifies are relevant to planning and management in higher education, several deserve special mention. Since we are in the knowledge business, it is especially significant that Naisbitt's first megatrend involves the transformation from an industrial society into an information society. According to Naisbitt, a U.S. Department of Commerce economist concluded that about two thirds of the economic growth in this country between 1948 and 1973 came about because of the increased size and education of the work force and the greater pool of knowledge available to workers. Furthermore, Naisbitt contends that innovations in communications and computer technology will accelerate the pace of change by collapsing the information float—the amount of time that information spends in the communications channel. The effect will be a rapid acceleration in the pace of change because of the elimination of delays in the information transmittal process. More significantly, he surmises that the new information technologies, although first applied to old industrial tasks, will give birth to new activities, processes, and products. The phrase *business as usual* became obsolete several years ago.

Today we are witnessing a remarkable acceleration of information transmittal and human communication on our campuses. Electronic mail is rapidly gaining acceptance by senior managers and faculty alike, because it saves vast amounts of time by eliminating the telephone tag so common to our academic lives. The potential benefit is greater in academe than it is in business, because few academics and students have access to support personnel who are available for message relay. Of even greater significance are the benefits to those who relay electronically entire texts of reports, policy papers, research findings, and so forth to colleagues for information, review, and comment. One of the most significant benefits is that this can be done asynchronously; that is, sender and receiver do not have to be engaged at the same time, and therefore both are free to select the optimum time for the activity. It is hard to describe the tremendous boost in both efficiency and effectiveness that this technology affords; many will not comprehend it until they have actually experienced it. The ultimate form of such communication is called *electronic computer conferencing,* and scholars are finding that some very important spatial and temporal impediments to the advance of knowledge have largely disappeared.

Stages of Technological Development

The transformation to a new societal norm does not happen instantaneously. Naisbitt (1982, p. 27) asserts that "there are three stages of technological development: First the new technology or innovation follows the line of least resistance; second, the technology is used to improve previous technologies (this stage can last a long time); and third, new directions or users are discovered that grow out of the technology itself."

When it was introduced in the late 1970s, the microcomputer was viewed as a hobbyist's toy and was initially used to do things that had previously been done on large mainframe computers. However, as friends, neighbors, and others began to see the ease with which certain time-consuming tasks could be done, the microcomputer gained in acceptance, and its applications became more widespread. The leap into the second stage came with the arrival of the electronic spreadsheet—a modern version of an ubiquitous tool—and with the advent of color presentation (as opposed to analytic) graphics applications. The inventors of the first electronic spreadsheet had difficulty explaining the value of their invention. The computer-illiterate thought that what was being offered as an advance was something that computers had always done, and they saw no increased benefit. The computer professionals were unimpressed, because the spreadsheet was not innovative insofar as computer technology was concerned. It was the middle managers who provided the transformation into the second stage of development. They immediately recognized that the electronic version was an orders-of-magnitude improvement on the existing paper-and-pencil technology. We are just entering the third stage in this specific development, which is part of an overall trend. Now, even the inventors are astonished at the uses being made of their brainchild. In many applications, however, higher education is still mired in the first stage of technological application as individuals experiment with the new force in their academic lives.

Other Pertinent Megatrends

Four other of Naisbitt's (1982) megatrends are of particular importance for those of us with a concern for the planning and management of colleges and universities: One is from centralization to decentralization, the second is from representative democracy to participatory democracy, the third is from hierarchies to networking, and the fourth is from institutional help to self-help. Naisbitt notes that both agricultural and information societies are decentralized: "Farmers could grow crops wherever the right field was; today you can start an information business with a telephone and a typewriter" (p. 98). One manifestation of this decentralization is the growing strength of local and special-interest subgroups of national trade and professional associations. For example, there are now nearly two dozen regional associations formally affiliated with the Association for Institutional Research, and many attract more than a hundred delegates to their regional meetings. But, even in our campus lives the new technology has made it less important that all participants be in the same location at the same time.

Decentralization, in this era, is closely related to increased opportunities for participatory democracy. This has altered the personal dynamics of meeting situations, and in some cases it has altered the decision outcome. Recently, at a private university in the Pacific Northwest, both the faculty and the students used electronic worksheets to construct detailed analyses and budget alternatives to the one proposed by the administration. Institutional budgeting became less centralized and more readily shaped and amended by decentralized interests.

According to Naisbitt, "For centuries, the pyramid structure was the way we organized and managed ourselves" (p. 189). However, hierarchical structures often impeded communication. Thus, networks developed for the sharing of ideas, information, and resources. With the rapid developments in computer and communications technology, persons with similiar interests can communicate instantly, even though they are physically and socially distant from one another. A dean at a Midwestern university decided he might like to buy one of the new lightweight lap-size portable microcomputers. He used a national electronic mail and conferencing service to enter a general query regarding the strengths and weaknesses of a particular model. Within hours, he received such extensive feedback that he knew more about the machine than the salesman at the local store. But, networks have even greater utility in the creation and exchange of knowledge and the forging of new ideas.

Self-help has always been a fundamental part of the American character. In recent years, though, it has taken on a new force to compensate for systems and organizations that have failed to live up to their promise. The new technology has permitted individuals to become increasingly independent —of intermediaries of "priesthoods" that communicate in arcane jargon—to accomplish their learning. For example, the Apple microcomputer was designed for the general public, not for specialists. As a result, special attention has been given to making systems and instructions as user-friendly as possible. With each passing day, major improvements are being made to simplify operations and improve the basic readability of instructions. The manager or professional now has a full and complete choice of deciding whether to engage in an activity or analysis directly or to delegate it to another.

The Third Wave of Societal Change

All ten megatrends specified by Naisbitt (1982) affect higher education and its role in society. But, the five just mentioned influence the planning and management of colleges and universities most directly. It is this overarching third wave of societal change, fundamentally intertwined with the development of microprocessor technology, to which college and university administrators must direct their attention. The wise selection of microware in all its forms—hard, soft, and firm—for intelligent and appropriate application is a time-consuming but eminently productive activity for higher education officials. We may hope that none will become victims of infotox—"the dark side of the computer revolution [consisting of] a new, insidious addiction and... an accompanying type of mental distress that we call Information Toxicity Syndrome" (Fridlund, 1983, p. 17). Fridlund prescribes some remedies that can alleviate acute symptoms on an individual basis. More to be feared, however, are the societal implications of infotox, because, if Fridlund is correct (p. 18), "they'll run wide and deep, [and] the bottleneck in the information revolution will not be hardware or software but the human being." You, the humanware engaged in planning and management, can affect the outcome in a positive and constructive manner.

References

Evans, C. *The Micro Millenium.* London: Viking, 1979.
Fridlund, A. J. "Information Toxicity." *PC World,* November 1983, pp. 17–18.
Naisbitt, J. *Megatrends: Ten New Directions Transforming Our Lives.* New York: Warner, 1982.
Stewart, T. R. "Personal Computers in the Corporate Environment." *The Week in Review,* 1983, *83* (36).
Toffler, A. *The Third Wave.* New York: Bantam, 1981.

William L. Tetlow is director of computing resources and director of the Management Products Division at the National Center for Higher Education Management Systems (NCHEMS).

Computer-based information systems have evolved from emphasizing data processing to providing full and flexible support for management.

The Changing Nature of Computer-Based Information Systems

Paul T. Brinkman

From specially equipped telephones to artificial intelligence, new modes of creating and handling information are everywhere around us. Not the least among these developments are the more versatile computer-based information systems (CBISs) designed to provide support for those who manage organizations.

The effort to provide greater management support through the CBIS has been going on for some time. Advances in computer technology have been a great stimulus, of course, but work in the behavioral sciences, applied mathematics, linguistics, and other disciplines has also helped to move the process along. Because so many factors have contributed to the development of the CBIS, some of the concepts and terminology, to say nothing of the underlying trends, may not be clear to all concerned. In this chapter, key terms and concepts in information systems are reviewed in relation to one another and to a varied background of changes over time, types of management activity, and roles that an information system can play in support of management. The emphasis throughout is on the intent of particular developments, the purposes they serve, and where they seem to be heading. The chapter ends with a discussion of the most dramatic recent development in CBISs: the emergence of the microcomputer. Because of microcomputing technology, CBISs have been evolving more rapidly and becoming more widespread than ever before. Indeed, new applications are occurring one after another and in nearly every conceivable situation. Because microcomputers are serving as a catalyst for many of these developments, they provide a forward-looking conclusion to this chronology of the evolution of CBIS.

Two fundamental trends in that evolution are noteworthy. One is a gradual increase in the types of managerial activity supported by CBISs. Managerial activities can be delineated in various ways, but Anthony's (1965) focus on levels of control best serves the present purposes. He distinguishes three levels: operational control, which is directed toward the accomplishment of specific tasks; management control or coordination, which is directed toward the accomplishment of organizational objectives; and strategic planning, which is directed toward the establishment of organizational objectives and policies. In carrying out each of these activities, managers make different demands on the information system, both in terms of what they require and of how they ask for it and want it delivered. For instance, at the operational control level, data must usually be highly disaggregated and quite current, whereas at the strategic level, useful data may be highly aggregated and not very current. Regular periodic reporting may serve management control needs well, but strategic planning typically requires much more of an ad hoc and flexible approach to the acquisition and use of information. Over time, the emphasis in CBISs has shifted. Initially, it was directed at supporting operations, but since then it has broadened to include coordination and, most recently, strategic planning as well.

A second trend has to do with a broadening of the kind of support that CBISs provide to managers. To summarize current thinking on the matter, a CBIS should be able to do three things in support of management: First, it should provide access to much of the data and information needed for making decisions and for understanding the workings of the organization. Second, it should provide a medium, or set of alternative media, that allows data and information to be assembled, manipulated, analyzed, and reported. Third, it should provide support for the thought processes, for the relating of assumptions, concepts, facts, rules of thumb, and so on that are required for managerial understanding and decision making. Thus, the initial emphasis on the provision of data has shifted over time to an ever increasing concern for information content, for appropriate media, and for ways of supporting thinking and reasoning.

Information Systems Concepts

Two basic terms in the lexicon of information systems are *data* and *information*. The terms are often used interchangeably, but in most cases there is value in distinguishing between them. *Data* refers to quantities or codes that arise out of observation and measurement. Thus, the attributes of data are the attributes of measurement: validity, reliability, and accuracy. In contrast, *information* is that which informs, that which in some way reduces uncertainty. The attributes of information may subsume those of data, but they also include such user-related attributes as timeliness, relevance, and acceptability.

Data become informative if and when they reduce uncertainty. The transformation of data into information cannot be taken for granted, as if the process occurs automatically. Effort is usually required. Fortunately, some of the new developments in information systems, in particular those relating to data structuring tools (for example, graphics and electronic spreadsheet programs), make it easier to transform data into information.

Another basic term is the word *system*. In the context of information systems, *system* refers to a network of structures and channels for recording, storing, retrieving, analyzing, and transferring data and information. No organization could function without some sort of system in that sense, but organizations differ considerably in the extent to which they are systematic, that is, regular, methodical, and formal in their approach. The concepts discussed later in this chapter reflect a series of developments aimed at helping organizations to become both more systematic with respect to data and information and more capable of responding to nonsystematic demands for those commodities.

Electronic Data Processing. The term *data processing* is relatively new, being associated largely with the computer age. However, the activity in question is much older. Indeed, some of the very earliest formal education that we know of was devoted to the training of scribes or record keepers. The Sumerians of 3000 B.C. compiled their records the hard way—they impressed them on clay tablets. Thanks to technology, things have gotten easier since then, although we have given up some durability. In any case, it is a long way from clay tablets to laser disks, electronic keyboards, touch screens, and voice-command systems. The development curve is a familiar one: dramatically exponential. In fact, the first practical alternatives to purely manual means of data processing—electromechanical and punched card devices—are of recent memory. Electronic data processing, which is the preferred, current alternative to hand processing, first appeared in the 1950s. Despite this enormous shift in operating modes and the increasingly rapid pace of development, however, the point of this effort remains much the same.

Thus, the term *electronic data processing* (EDP) refers to an electronic system that processes—that is, that records, stores, maintains, and recalls—data pertinent to the basic operation of an organization. The data typically are records of transactions and other events that recur, such as paying vendors, receiving donations, registering students, checking out library books, and so on. In short, EDP facilitates and to some extent automates clerical tasks, including the production of low-level (nonintegrated) summary reports. This kind of data processing was the dominant focus of the first era of CBISs and it remains a fundamental component of many such systems.

Management Information Systems. By the early 1960s, it had become apparent that organizations would do well to put more time and effort into organizing their data and information resources in ways that could serve management coordination needs more directly. Hence, the era of management information systems (MISs) began. By connotation at least, MISs are information- rather than data-oriented. They are geared to the production of a series of reports that enables managers to assess how well the organization is meeting its objectives. Monthly budget reports, course enrollment reports, and reports showing the number of majors by discipline or the cost per student credit-hour by department are examples of MIS products in higher education institutions.

Comprehensive data bases, interrelationships among data files, and highly structured information flows are the focus of the MIS. In developing a MIS, considerable attention is paid to the needs analysis, that is, to determining what managers need to know and when. A MIS can be developed for a particular area: In higher education, the admissions and recruiting area is often a prime target; in business, marketing may have a separate MIS. A MIS can also be organization-wide, which usually means that all major areas are covered and that there is some integration among them within the reporting system. In either case, MIS developers typically aim at comprehensiveness.

This is not to say that all data elements thought to be important will reside in electronic form or that all reporting will be automated but rather that all important data elements and reports will be accounted for somewhere in the system. It may be worth noting that, contrary to EDP, MISs have no inherent relationship to computers or to any other electronic devices. In its pure form a MIS is first a conceptual, logical entity, which then is operationalized in whatever ways are available and preferable. In many instances, of course, the MIS ends up being primarily computer-based.

Little doubt has been expressed as to whether MISs are useful for middle managers, but there has been a feeling, apparently widespread, that MISs are typically not very helpful to senior managers (Zeleny, 1982). It has also been generally acknowledged that the typical MIS application concentrates on objective structures and ignores the particular, idiosyncratic needs of individual managers. For example, the same monthly budget report format usually goes to all department heads no matter how differently each of them might like to see the data presented and analyzed. Similarly, there is a tendency for MISs to be rigid and to focus on routine reporting. It usually takes considerable effort to create a MIS, and the creators have little inclination to change the system once it is finally in operation. Whether these characteristics of existing MISs are intrinsic to the MIS concept is moot. Sprague and Carlson (1982) discuss the matter. What is clear is that the perceived characteristics have encouraged the development of other approaches to the management and use of data and information in support of management.

Data Base Management Systems. One such approach is the data base management system (DBMS). The term is loosely defined, partly because of the proliferation in microcomputer software. Occasionally, software vendors refer to their products as DBMSs when file handlers would be closer to the mark. Generally speaking, a DBMS is a set of software programs that at a minimum allows users to organize, maintain, and query data files and to generate custom-designed reports from those files. There is a considerable range between the capabilities of personal DBMSs that run on microcomputers and mainframe-based, highly sophisticated DBMSs.

DBMSs are said to be in their fourth generation at the present time. The term itself is not as old as the genealogy might imply, but the underlying issues have been present since at least the beginning of EDP. By the mid 1970s, the DBMS had come into prominence as a tool to enhance both the data entry and maintenance side of a CBIS as well as its ability to respond to new and ad hoc demands for data retrieval. Data retrieval is particularly important for management support. Managers frequently need to retrieve novel sets of data from their organization's data base, and the items requested often are located in different data files. The novel data set may be intended as a new (but henceforth routine) report in the institution's information system, or it may become part of a one-time personal analysis. Whatever the intended use, the problem is the same. The data need to be found, extracted, and formatted appropriately—and it ought not to take six months to do this. A good DBMS permits these tasks to be done quickly, perhaps even without the direct assistance of a computer professional. A MIS that is developed in conjunction with a good DBMS is far more able to meet the particular or nonroutine data needs of managers than a MIS that must contend with compartmentalized data files, inadequate report generators, and the like.

The DBMS computer programs that provide the required integration among data files and elements thereof can incorporate rather different strategies. Such terms as *hierarchical, network,* and *relational* describe some of the alternative ways in which elements in the data base can be connected. These terms often become part of the name or the description of a particular DBMS. The technicalities involved in the alternative strategies are beyond the scope of this chapter. An excellent discussion can be found in Kruglinski (1983).

Modeling. The use of models is another development that can be thought of as enhancing the traditional, highly structured MIS. When used in an information systems context, the term *model* usually means some type of representation of reality. This is also true in science, where models have been used for centuries. The semantic issue is not as straightforward as it might seem, however. For instance, despite its long lineage, usage of the term *model* in science has been said to be "confusing and often confused" (Kaplan, 1964, p. 267). The same could be said for the word *theory,* which on occasion is used as a synonym for *model*. Presumably, the manifold nature of reality and the many ways in which it can be represented are at fault.

In any case, the ambiguity of the term *model* surfaces quickly when we try to understand how it is used in a management context. For instance, some writers argue that any spreadsheet application is a model (Gabel, 1983). Others apply the term to virtually any identifiable group of mathematical or logical calculations (Sprague and Carlson, 1982). For still others, the term conjures up images of complex systems of assumptions, initial conditions, and relationships (Hopkins and Massy, 1981). There is not much that can be done to reduce this confusion in our common parlance other than to use stipulative definitions in situations where ambiguity might be harmful.

At the least, however, model is typically used to refer to explicit representations of reality. Individuals frequently employ mental models—rough, implicit theories of how things work, of why things are the way they are. But, these implicit constructs must be made explicit before they can become models in a more limited and precise sense of the term. In other words, while models are indeed representations of reality, it is important to add the qualifying phrase, *as that reality is understood.* It is interesting to note that in basic science models are used primarily to enhance understanding. In management, they are normally used to support decision making. Yet, one of the frequently reported benefits of using models in higher education management is greater understanding (Bloomfield and Updegroove, 1982). The additional understanding comes by and large from being more explicit about how the institution and its many constituents function.

Two types of mathematical models are used frequently in support of management decision making. In *optimization models,* mathematical formulations and calculations are used to find optimal solutions: The model looks at a number of parameters and picks the best value or values to optimize some result. Deciding how much of each of several products to produce in order to maximize profits is a typical optimization problem in the business sector. In higher education, such highly structured problems are harder to find, but it is conceivable, for instance, that some portion of institutional student aid might be distributed in accord with an optimization model.

Simulation models are used much more frequently in higher education. They represent situations in such a way that the effects of varying a particular parameter value or formulation can be ascertained. For example, a typical use of a simulation model would be to look at trade-offs between the amount of a faculty pay raise and the number of faculty that could be employed, given certain constraints. Such models can also be used to determine the sensitivity of a particular solution to the various parameters and the operating characteristics of the solution. For instance, the results of a model used to balance university revenues and expenditures might be quite sensitive to forecast levels of enrollment. If the forecasts are produced by a model, they, too, will have sensitivities that might be worth investigating. Most of the what-if and how-to (goal-seeking) analyses that have become so widespread in recent years involve some type of simulation modeling.

Increasingly, institutional information systems are likely to include a formal modeling capability and probably several varieties thereof; for recent examples, see Hopkins and others (1982) and Timm (1983). Much of the data that are likely to be used in a model will already reside in the system. Furthermore, the direct results of the modeling activity are themselves items of information that normally belong somewhere in the information system. When a modeling capability is added to a traditional MIS, the resulting system has much greater potential to meet the information needs of individuals responsible for strategic planning, and, whatever the level of management activity, a modeling capability provides a form of intellectual support that can assist managers in getting the most out of the information that is available.

Decision Support Systems. A discussion of the ongoing effort to overcome the management support limitations of the typical MIS leads naturally to the decision support system (DSS). The term *decision support system* was used infrequently until the late 1970s, but it now turns up often in both scholarly and popular media. It usually refers to an interactive computer-based system that helps decision makers use data and models to solve relatively unstructured problems. Although it is obvious that decisions can be made by means other than computer-based systems, the link with computers is one of the common elements in what is otherwise a somewhat loose term. That linkage reflects the roots that DSSs have in the work done on interactive computing at the Massachusetts Institute of Technology in the 1960s. Other DSS roots go back to the efforts of Simon (1977) in the 1950s to distinguish between programmable and nonprogrammable tasks or problems. The terms *structured, semistructured,* and *unstructured* are more in vogue today, but the idea is the same, and so is the implication that different types of information technologies are needed for the three types of tasks. Whereas the typical MIS may be a useful tool for routine, well-structured problems, it is less helpful in handling semistructured or unstructured problems. For those kinds of problems, something new is needed, something more flexible, more under the control of the user, more precisely attuned to differences in cognitive style and to the particular decisions that managers must make; the needed new focus has been labeled the *decision support system* (DSS).

While not all theorists and developers agree, many argue that DSSs are directed most properly toward the needs of senior management. Senior managers are the most likely to be confronted with relatively unstructured, ill-defined problems that involve a strategic rather than a tactical or operational perspective, problems that can change quickly, and problems that may require external data (that is, data not derivable from the organization's operational data base). These characteristics describe the problems and decisions that clearly are the targets for most DSS developers. But, since managers other than those at the highest organizational levels occasionally experience the same kinds of problems, the focus of the DSS on the needs of senior management is probably better viewed as a matter of emphasis and degree than as categorical.

DSSs are not being designed as replacements for MISs or for EDP. Basic transaction processing and production of routine management reports are vital to any organization. There is widespread agreement that DSSs are likely to be most effective and most easily developed and maintained when they are designed to work in conjunction with other processes and systems as part of an overall information system.

Supportive Research

There are many disciplines and fields of study that in one way or another enhance our understanding of information-related issues and technologies. The disciplines and fields discussed in this section have led or are leading to developments that are directly supportive of management, primarily by aiding the thought processes of managers.

Operations Research and Management Science. Operations research (OR) began during World War II. Britain's employment of scientists in the effort to operationalize an antiaircraft radar system provided the initial impetus. As the war went on, scientific analysis was directed not only at weapons development and use but at a variety of management tasks known as *logistics*—the procurement, distribution, maintenance, and replacement of materiel and personnel. After the war, the increasingly complex and far-flung nature of large corporations spurred continued develoment of OR and its use in the private sector.

Management science (MS) has come to be a generally equivalent term for operations research (OR) in the United States, although it appears to be somewhat broader in scope. Both terms refer to systematic efforts to solve organizational problems using formalized, mathematical routines that typically are optimization models of some kind, although simulation models are also employed. Inventory control (how much, what mix of products, and so on) is typical of the problems addressed by OR/MS in the industrial sector. The need to meet customer demand in a timely fashion must be balanced against the need to restrict the amount of capital tied up in inventory. Other general types of OR/MS problems include allocation, queuing, sequencing and routing, replacement and maintenance, search, and competition (Rivett, 1980).

It appears that the impact of OR/MS in business and industry has thus far been less than expected. There has been too much emphasis on technique and too little attention to data issues and to the unstructured nature of many management problems (Zeleny, 1982). The same problem has been noted with regard to OR/MS in higher education (Hopkins and Schroeder, 1977). What is interesting in the present context is that some OR/MS advocates see a new opportunity for the powerful analytical techniques of the DSS movement to become useful management tools. At the very least, it is clear that the developing medium for DSS—the hardware and software—will make OR/MS routines far more readily available than they were in the past.

Multicriteria Decision Making. A term that relates to both OR/MS and

DSS is *multicriteria decision making* (MCDM). MCDM has roots in mathematical and operations research techniques that began in the 1950s, but the techniques and the underlying concerns for decision making did not come together as a field of study until the late 1960s. Whether MCDM is best thought of as a part of OR/MS or as a separate field of study is debatable and will only be resolved over time. The MCDM viewpoint contrasts sharply with classical or OR/MS decision analysis, which focuses on single-criterion decision making. In classical OR/MS, optimization is achieved by selecting the best alternative with respect to a single, predefined criterion. In contrast, MCDM focuses on attributes at work and in which no single goal, objective, or attribute dominates. MCDM is based on a realistic description of how decisions are made, while classical OR/MS is grounded in a conception of how decisions ought to be made. Yet, MCDM retains a strong commitment to rigorous analysis as a vital component of the process. According to Keen (1977), MCDM's position on decision making is somewhere between just muddling through and the classical optimization view.

The ultimate fate of MCDM probably depends on whether a suitable calculus can be developed that will take the analyst and manager beyond the mere recognition that some decisions involve multiple criteria. Calculation techniques are in fact being developed: The evaluative portions of decision making, the rating and ranking aspects, have been the focus of investigative attention. The strategy that seems to be taking hold features an interactive approach in which the formal decision aid assists the decision maker to clarify assumptions and preferences and to achieve greater cognitive control over the various components of the decision process. In terms of Simon's (1977) three stages in that process, the goal of optimization seems to be shifting away from choice and toward intelligence and design. Clearly, there is some congruence between this strategy and the basic themes underlying the DSS approach.

Those who build MCDM decision aids have not abandoned the choice stage entirely. A consensus has developed that favors the use of hybrid models in which one acknowledges both the ideal solution and some type of satisfying rule; the ideal solution has a role to play in the model, but the goal of the analysis is to find the best possible solution given the circumstances (Keen, 1977). However, finding the best solution requires the interactive approach described earlier. Thus, the emphasis remains on supporting the decision maker, on aiding rather than on replacing human judgment.

Artificial Intelligence. The term *artificial intelligence* (AI) dates from the 1950s. The advent of the electronic computer late in the 1940s soon gave rise to the hope that various mental activities, especially those relating to problem solving, might be performed by a machine. After several decades of research, *artificial intelligence* remains a somewhat ambiguous term, partly because *intelligence* is, too. More fundamentally, there are basic disagreements among those who work in the field about the goal of AI. There is considerable difference, for instance, between simulating a logical thought process on a computer and building a computer that can somehow think for itself.

Research on AI is carried on primarily in cognitive psychology and computer science but also in linguistics, philosophy, cybernetics, and pattern recognition studies. The research may seem arcane and unrelated to management support needs, but in fact much of what we take for granted today about computer capabilities came out of AI research labs. Interactive computing is an example, as are robotics and programmable automation. More is on the way. Three terms to look for in this context are *expert systems, natural language processing,* and *fuzzy sets.*

Expert systems, occasionally referred to as *knowledge engineering systems,* imitate the decision-making processes and problem-solving skills of experts in various disciplines. The resulting computer programs are said to be the most ambitious and successful AI applications thus far (Garfield, 1983). The programs include facts, heuristic knowledge (rules of thumb), and inference procedures that link facts and heuristics with particular problems.

The expert systems developed to date are focused on limited domains of issues and problems. Limitation in that sense is a key to their success. It has turned out to be easier to model the reasoning processes of specialists than it is to model common sense inferences, even those of a child (Duda and Shortliffe, 1983). Thus, there are expert systems that identify the chemical structure of unknown compounds, that assist doctors in diagnosing and treating disease, that locate geological structures likely to contain oil, and that solve algebra problems, but there are none, it appears, that might render assistance to a general manager.

Developments in expert systems are likely to be very substantial in the near future, however, and more generalizable types of systems may be forthcoming. Still, expert systems typically involve a closed-world assumption in which the problem domain is highly circumscribed, and to some extent they are designed to replace human judgment. As such, they may be less suitable to the changing world of the manager than the more open-ended DSSs that are designed to assist rather than to replace human judgment.

So-called natural language processing programs offer new opportunities for those who do not have the time to learn special languages in order to communicate with computers. In the natural language (NL) approach, the operator uses everyday language to input information. Some of the programs now under development rely on pattern recognition techniques for responding to commands that are unique to each person who inputs information. Thus, not only is the user-machine interface simplified, it is also personalized.

Although natural language programs are at the forefront of much information systems research today, interest in them started very early in the history of computers. In the 1950s, for instance, there was great interest in developing machines that could translate text, especially Russian scientific journals. That effort largely failed, foundering on an overly simplistic view of language. During the 1960s, Chomsky's linguistic theories helped to build a stronger foundation for the NL approach, and Wizenbaum created some notoriety for NL with ELIZA, an interactive program that mimicked the nondirective responses of a particular counseling technique. While ELIZA merely reacted to key words and converted the response into another question, most attempts at NL processing since then have focused on programs that in some more fundamental way determine the meaning of words and sentences. In this sense, NL processing is one of the core issues in AI. At a more immediately practical level, some of today's current interest in NL processing is motivated by the desire to make computers easier to use.

The concept of fuzzy sets originated in control systems theory in the 1960s. Some authors are convinced that it can play a substantive role in organizational information systems designed to lend decision support (Negoita, 1983). A fuzzy set lacks well-defined criteria for determining whether an object does or does not belong to it. Fuzzy sets are anything but trivial in human affairs. As Zeleny (1982, p. 158) puts it, "the key elements in human thinking are not numbers but labels of fuzzy sets, that is, classes of objects in which the transition from membership to nonmembership is gradual rather than abrupt." The way we use a label, such as *red,* to designate a color illustrates the point. The label is imprecise as to class membership, yet it is both significant and useful. Few would argue that it would be better, in ordinary human affairs, to apply instead the numerical value of the appropriate wavelength—even though the second approach would be more precise. In other words, then, fuzzy set theory implies a recognition that usefulness and precision can be incompatible.

With respect to models that support decision making, the fuzzy set notion is made operational through the inclusion of linguistic (qualitative) variables, such as *good* or *profitable,* instead of relying entirely on variables that express choice preferences only in either/or terms. This inclusion of linguistic variables in DSS models permits expression in a more natural language, allowing for approximate reasoning and for a more explicit consideration of professional expertise and judgment (Negoita, 1983). The challenge facing fuzzy set theorists is to develop a mathematical language that will in fact make all that possible.

Given the emphasis on linguistic variables, it is not surprising that fuzzy sets and MCDM are said to be intimately related (Blin, 1977) or that fuzzy set theory is said to provide a framework in which models for MCDM can be constructed (Yager, 1982). Similarly, techniques for handling linguistic variables should be useful in the development of what at least one author has called right-brained DSS (Young, 1983). These DSSs are directed toward tasks that are essentially qualitative and creative in nature, such as conceptualizing new products or formulating general policy, as opposed to tasks that primarily involve logical reasoning and computation—processes attributed by some investigators to the left side of the human brain.

Cognitive Psychology. From a management support perspective, some of the research in cognitive psychology bears mentioning. Of particular importance is the research that has established differences among individuals in cognitive style. This research has provided much of the rationale for designing DSSs that are flexible, that is, adaptable to individual preferences in the handling of data and knowledge representations of various kinds (Robey, 1983). There is some question whether research on cognitive style will lead to more specific design criteria for DSSs (Huber, 1983). Nonetheless, valuable insights have been gained regarding both the cognitive styles of managers (McKenney and Keen, 1974) and the problems encountered in converting data into information (Hackman, 1983).

Research on pattern recognition has also provided a basis for information systems design. A key finding is that graphic presentation, as opposed to tabular presentation, can enhance the rate and quantity of information transfer. Considerable progress has already been made on the details needed for making practical use of this discovery. Techniques for effective graphic presentations have been compiled (for example, Schmid and Schmid, 1979), and a management information system based on graphic presentations has been designed (Jarett, 1983). Currently, both the software and the hardware for computer business graphics are undergoing explosive growth. In all likelihood, graphics will play an increasingly important role in future CBISs.

Microcomputers and CBISs

In the foregoing discussion, I proposed that a CBIS can support management decision making by providing a medium for the analysis of data and information, assistance for managerial thinking, and access to data and information. The microcomputer is contributing heavily to management support in all three ways.

The term *automation* has long been associated with computers, relating mostly to clerical and production tasks. Microcomputers are hastening the day when the term *mediation* will also be associated with computers. Word processing programs, for instance, provide the user with a medium that is conducive to working with words. From the management perspective, mediation is even more clearly represented in the graphics capabilities that microcomputer hardware and software are now helping to make widely available. Whether it be analytical graphics or so-called presentation graphics, the situation is the same. Some individuals find value in working with data in an alternative medium — either to learn more themselves or to present the material in such a way that others can grasp it more readily. When numerical relationships are graphed, they take on a sensory presence, a perceptible form that is missing from tabular presentations, allowing an individual to see the relationships differently or perhaps for the first time ever. The ubiquitous electronic spreadsheet can also be thought of as a kind of medium, a vehicle within which certain types of analysis not only become easier but are more likely to lead to insight.

It is perhaps worth noting that word processing, graphics, and electronic spreadsheets have all been given a tremendous impetus by small, desktop computers. In terms of wide-scale use of these tools, large computers are following rather than leading. In fact, electronic spreadsheets were designed initially for microcomputers, and they were not available on larger systems until their utility had been demonstrated on the small systems. This is not meant to disparage large computers but merely to note the order of development—and to reinforce the notion that desktop computers involve far more than miniaturization. In general, it is counterproductive to think of microcomputers as small versions of large computers. Without belaboring the point, it is hard to overemphasize the difference between a desktop device that can become an extension of one's self akin to the artist's palette and brush and a device that under someone else's direction supplies management reports, however informative and necessary those reports may be. Of course, the microcomputer can also take the form of a terminal, which in effect converts a properly equipped large computer into the new kind of tool.

A primary role for microcomputers in supporting human thought processes is to make certain types of computer-based analytical tools more widely available. High-level modeling languages and the mathematical models of OR/MS have been available on large computers for some time. In these instances, desktop computers are following rather than leading. However, as they become more powerful, they make these analytical tools more readily accessible to a wider range of managers, often in a format that is in today's jargon more user-friendly. As for AI, the implication of the massive effort entailed in building the so-called fifth generation of computers (in pursuit of a very ambitious formulation of AI) seems to be that desktop computers are out of the picture in that field for the foreseeable future. However, if we adopt a modest and more incremental view of AI, then it can be argued that desktop computers are already very much part of applied AI. So-called templates, essentially dedicated electronic worksheets, are already providing managers with a growing range of applications that have intelligence embedded in them; for example, cash flow analysis, amortization schedules, space utilization programs, and the like. Expert systems, a considerable leap ahead on the AI continuum, are just now becoming available on microcomputers. Natural language query systems with substantial flexibility are also near at hand (Greene, 1984). Extensions of word processing, so-called idea processors, that assist individuals to organize their thoughts are another modest but eminently practical tool that is just now becoming available on microcomputers (Bonner, 1984).

However sophisticated the media and the models for decision support become, managers will, of course, continue to require appropriate access to data and information. Microcomputers have at least three useful roles to play in the provision of data and information: as the host computer for a modest-size data base; as a terminal with respect to one or more information systems—a place where data can be entered and retrieved and where messages can be sent and received; and as a place where internal and external data or, more generally, system and nonsystem data can be merged for ready display and analysis.

Microcomputers are truly useful tools that can support management in all the basic ways. Managers at all levels are likely to find legitimate uses for them. Yet, they are not the solution to all information system problems. In some instances, they can end up becoming part of the problem rather than the solution. For institutions that are plagued with separate, disconnected data bases or that cannot generate the basic information that managers need routinely, a handful of microcomputers can increase the number of detached, islandlike data sets—the time-consuming end runs—a situation sometimes referred to as *closet computing* by the computer professional. Like other tools, microcomputers are most useful when they are carefully integrated into a larger system. In the long run, there is really no good alternative to ensuring that the basic information system components—the data elements, data structures and relationships, information flows, and so on—have been properly and adequately dealt with. Computer technology has already developed beyond our ability to use it to maximum advantage. Too much emphasis on any one tool will serve only to widen the gap.

Summary

Over the past several decades, CBISs have become increasingly supportive of management. While the earlier systems focused on the needs of managers closest to everyday operations, the newer systems are being designed for the manager with broader, more long-range responsibilities. CBISs have moved from the automation of clerical tasks to summative reporting to being a versatile, flexible tool for decision support. They have moved from providing mere data to providing the means for transforming data into information to providing a versatile medium for representing knowledge wherein managers can analyze data, formulate ideas, structure arguments, and build models. In addition, the knowledge that was once the sole preserve of the computer specialist is gradually being embedded directly in the system itself, where it is immediately available to the manager. For most of the history of CBISs, the technical requirements of the hardware and software have been a dominant consideration. We are now entering a period in which the requirements of the end user will be dominant. Computer-based information systems are now learning to speak the language of the manager. No one yet knows whether decision making under these new conditions will produce better decisions, but the process will surely be different.

References

Anthony, R. *Planning and Control Systems: A Framework for Analysis.* Cambridge, Mass.: Harvard Business School, 1965.

Blin, J. M. "Fuzzy Sets in Multiple Criteria Decision Making." In M. K. Starr and M. Zeleny (Eds.), *Multiple Criteria Decision Making.* TIMS Studies in the Management Sciences, Vol. 6. Amsterdam: North Holland, 1977.

Bloomfield, S. D., and Updegrove, D. A. "Modeling for Insight, Not Numbers." *EDUCOM Bulletin,* 1982, *17,* (3), 5-9.

Bonner, P. "Enter, the Powerful New Idea Tools." *Personal Computing,* 1984, *8* (1), 70-79.

Duda, R. O., and Shortliffe, E. H. "Expert Systems Research." *Science,* 1983, *220,* 261–268.

Gabel, D. "'What If' You Build a Model?" *Personal Computing,* 1983, *7* (10), 82–93.

Garfield, E. "Artificial Intelligence: Using Computers to Think About Thinking. Part 2: Some Practical Applications of AI." *Current Contents/Social and Behavioral Sciences,* 1983, *15* (52), 5–17.

Greene, J. O. "Making Computers Smarter." *Popular Computing,* 1984, 96, 107.

Hackman, J. D. "Seven Maxims for Institutional Researchers: Applying Cognitive Theory and Research." *Research in Higher Education,* 1983, *18* (2), 195–208.

Hopkins, D. S. P., Lawrence, L. L., Sonenstein, B., and Tschectelin, J. D. "Financial Modeling: Four Success Stories." *EDUCOM Bulletin,* 1982, *17* (3), 11–16.

Hopkins, D. S. P., and Massy, W. F. *Planning Models for Colleges and Universities.* Stanford, Calif.: Stanford University Press, 1981.

Hopkins, D. S. P., and Schroeder, R. G. "Editors' Notes." In D. S. P. Hopkins and R. G. Schroeder (Eds.), *Applying Analytic Methods to Planning and Management.* New Directions for Institutional Research, no. 13. San Francisco: Jossey-Bass, 1977.

Huber, G. P. "Cognitive Style as a Basis for Designing MIS and DSS: Much Ado About Nothing?" *Management Science,* 1983, *29* (5), 567–579.

Jarett, I. M. *Computer Graphics and Reporting Financial Data.* New York: Wiley, 1983.

Kaplan, A. *The Conduct of Inquiry.* San Francisco: Chandler, 1964.

Keen, P. G. W. "The Evolving Concept of Optimality." In M. K. Starr and M. Zeleny (Eds.), *Multiple Criteria Decision Making.* TIMS Studies in the Management Sciences, Vol. 6. Amsterdam: North Holland, 1977.

Kruglinski, D. "Data Base Management Systems." *Popular Computing,* 1983, *2* (12), 116–134.

McKenney, J. L., and Keen, P. G. W. "How Managers' Minds Work." *Harvard Business Review,* 1974, *52* (3), 74–90.

Negoita, C. V. "Fuzzy Sets in Decision Support Systems." *Human Systems Management,* 1983, *4* (1), 27–33.

Rivett, P. *Model Building for Decision Analysis.* New York: Wiley, 1980.

Robey, D. "Cognitive Style and DSS Design: A Comment on Huber's Paper." *Management Science,* 1983, *29* (5), 580–582.

Schmid, C., and Schmid, S. *Handbook of Graphic Presentation.* New York: Wiley, 1979.

Simon, H. A. *The New Science of Management Decision.* (2nd ed.) Englewood Cliffs, N.J.: Prentice-Hall, 1977.

Sprague, R. H., Jr., and Carlson, E. D. *Building Effective Decision Support Systems.* Englewood Cliffs, N.J.: Prentice-Hall, 1982.

Timm, N. H. "Developing a Management Support System in Higher Education." *Planning for Higher Education,* 1983, *11* (2), 27–33.

Yager, R. R. "An Introduction to Applications of Possibility Theory." *Human Systems Management,* 1982, *3* (4), 246–253.

Young, L. F. "Computer Support for Creative Decision Making: Right-Brained DSS." In H. G. Sol (Ed.), *Processes and Tools for Decision Support.* Amsterdam: North Holland, 1983.

Zeleny, M. *Multiple Criteria Decision Making.* New York: McGraw-Hill, 1982.

Paul T. Brinkman is a senior associate at the National Center for Higher Education Management Systems in Boulder, Colorado, where he specializes in higher education finance, comparative data issues, and decision support systems.

Institutional researchers will find a wealth of useful applications for microcomputers and telecommunications, but they must be prepared for the changes that these new technologies will bring.

Using Microcomputers for Institutional Research

J. Lloyd Suttle

Judith, the director of institutional research, arrived at her office around 8:15 A.M. Using the microcomputer at her desk as a remote terminal, she logged onto the university's mainframe computer to check the status of a job she had run overnight in order to take advantage of discounts for third shift computing. She scanned the results of her statistical analyses, quickly performed two additional analyses using interactive SAS, and directed all the output to the high-speed line printer in a room down the hall where several offices shared it. Next, she checked her electronic mailbox and discovered two items: a note from the associate provost proposing a meeting for the following afternoon—she immediately responded that she could attend—and a memo from the admissions office requesting information for a questionnaire, which she asked her staff assistant to provide.

Judith spent the rest of the morning reviewing the printouts from the analyses that she had run earlier, extracting certain information and putting it into a file on her microcomputer. She later transferred this file from her microcomputer to the university's mainframe computer and then, via BITNET, to a data base containing comparative information from a number of different colleges and universities that was stored in a computer at another institution. She also shipped a copy of the complete data base to the mainframe at her own institution and, after some minor editing, input these data directly into a planning model running on her microcomputer using Lotus 1-2-3.

Judith spent her afternoon working on a paper that she and a colleague from another institution planned to present at the upcoming AIR forum. Using her microcomputer as a word processor, she merged the sections she had written with those that her colleague sent via TELENET, made a few revisions, and shipped them back to him before she went home. She included a note saying that, since the deadline for submitting the paper was fast approaching, she planned to prepare the tables and graphs for the paper that evening.

This scenario, while imaginary, is well within the capabilities of a growing number of institutional researchers. It illustrates the potential for increasingly widespread and wide-ranging applications of microcomputers for institutional research and planning. Many of these applications are examined in this chapter. Yet, no list can be comprehensive or exhaustive, for the technology is changing so rapidly and it is so flexible that its usefulness is limited only by the imagination and resourcefulness of users.

The Evolution of Computing and Institutional Research

On most campuses, the functions of institutional research are bound so inextricably to the use of computing that the terms *institutional research* and *computing* have become virtually synonymous in the minds of many administrators. The very definition of institutional research—"to provide information which supports institutional planning, policy formulation, and decision making" (Saupe, 1981, p. 1)—suggests its critical dependence on information processing technology. It is more than coincidence, therefore, that the ever increasing technological sophistication of institutional research has closely paralleled developments in information processing technology.

The use of microcomputers represents the next logical step in this process of simultaneous evolution. As many campuses enter what Mann (1982) has termed the second wave of computerization—a wave marked by smaller, less expensive, and much more widely available computers; a broader and somewhat less technically sophisticated community of users; and faster, less controlled growth—this evolution continues apace. The widespread use of microcomputers by institutional researchers has affected and will continue to affect not only how they do their jobs but what they do and what skills are necessary or important.

Besides changing the ways we manage our institutions, microcomputers should prove to be no exception.

Current and Potential Applications

The ability to gather, store, retrieve, analyze, integrate, and disseminate data lies at the core of the institutional research function. Even more important, however, is the ability to translate this information into a form that can be used for management decision making and planning. Microcomputers are particularly useful in this regard, for they allow data to be manipulated quickly and easily and to be presented in a wide range of forms.

To date, institutional researchers have barely scratched the surface of this new technology. A search of the ERIC data base on higher education in October 1983 revealed that, of the more than 2,200 entries pertaining to microcomputers, only seven pertained to the use of microcomputers for institutional research and planning. Nevertheless, a list of potential uses of microcomputers resembles a list of the functions typical of an office of institutional research.

No simple inventory is available of the many ways in which microcomputers, telecommunications, and other recent advances in information processing technology can enter into the functions of institutional research. A list of some of the present uses and coming extensions of this technology would recognize the microcomputer as a calculator with the capacity to collate large amounts of information and perform complex logical and mathematical operations in fractions of a second; as a tutor providing computer-assisted instruction, drill, and practice; as a laboratory in which computer simulations present analogues to management and planning exercises; as a blackboard on which information can be displayed graphically for a wide range of purposes; as a library in which enormous amounts of information can be stored efficiently and retrieved rapidly; as a telephone with which people can be drawn together to work on common or interrelated tasks; and, last but not least, as a typewriter that is changing the nature of the composing and editing of written material (Johnson, 1981). In all these applications, many institutional researchers will find that the microcomputer leads to greater efficiency in everything they do, especially in the two most essential and critical elements of their jobs: thinking and communicating.

Five applications of microcomputers directly support the major information needs of managers: word processing, numerical analysis, graphics, telecommunications, and data management. As this section shows, each of these applications can prove of immediate value to the institutional researcher.

Word Processing. The preparation of memos, reports, and correspondence is an essential and time-consuming component of every institutional researcher's job. Thus, it is not surprising that one of the first and most common applications of microcomputers has been word processing. By now, virtually everyone is familiar with the functions and efficacy of automated word processing, and some form of office automation has appeared in the vast majority of institutions. According to Mann (1982), this technology is beginning to revolutionize university offices. Furthermore, as word processing software becomes more powerful and flexible, microcomputers have begun to replace both stand-alone word processors and mainframe computers (that is, timesharing systems) as the dominant hardware for word processing.

The ability quickly and easily to enter, delete, reorganize, and revise textual information can produce two kinds of benefits: increased productivity (clerical savings, possibly resulting in cost reductions) and improved quality of written communications. Whether and to what extent these benefits are realized depends largely on how and by whom the word processor is used. For example, if it is used primarily by clerical staff in the way that typewriters have always been used, then the impact of the new technology will be limited. There will be some productivity improvements, since most typists will discover that they can type faster on a word processor than they can on a typewriter, and there are obvious benefits of using a word processor for documents that are revised and retyped one or more times. Furthermore, even if the word processor is used only by clerical staff, it will result in some improvement in writing quality, since the authors of memos and reports will feel less inhibited about revising their documents (perhaps even for a second or third time) if they know their changes can be made quickly, easily, and with far less irritation to staff than if the whole document has to be retyped. Yet, it is unlikely in such a situation that the benefits of automated word processing will outweigh its substantial costs.

The most significant benefits of word processing in an institutional research office will be realized when this new technology is used not just by the clerical staff as fancy typewriters but by professional staff as an alternative to typewriters. By using a microcomputer to compose and edit memos and reports, most institutional researchers will discover that they are able to improve not only the quality of their writing but also the clarity and cogency of their thinking. Writing with a word processor will, of course, require new skills (Zinsser, 1983), but most institutional researchers will discover that these skills are rather easy to acquire, especially when they begin to use microcomputers for a wide range of applications in addition to word processing. Finally, it is only when institutional researchers become facile in the use of word processing that they will be able to take full advantage of the microcomputer as a tool for accessing, translating, and communicating information.

In summary, while there are significant potential benefits to be realized from computerized word processing, those benefits are not guaranteed, and they may be accompanied by hidden costs. Word processing must therefore be implemented in the same way as any other major change in an organization—with caution as to its unintended consequences, with concern for its impact on the people involved, and with a willingness to adapt to unforeseen personal or situational factors.

Numerical Analysis. The analysis and reporting of quantitative information has been the stock-in-trade of institutional research since its beginning. Two types of software have been developed for microcomputers to facilitate numerical analysis. One is a set of packages designed to perform statistical analyses similar to those done by institutional researchers for years on mainframe computers. Since statistical analyses generally require large amounts of internal memory and are applied frequently to large data sets, statistical packages for microcomputers are a relatively recent development, and they are still somewhat limited in their capabilities. However, as faster and more powerful microprocessors, large-capacity fixed disks, and larger internal memories become available, institutional researchers will be able to shift an increasing share of their statistical analyses from mainframes to microcomputers. Microcomputers may never fully replace mainframes for statistical analysis, but there are many applications, such as the preparation of descriptive statistics on small data sets, where microcomputers are better suited than mainframes. And, microcomputers offer greater security than large multiuser systems, such as campus mainframe computers. This can prove to be an important advantage for the analysis of highly confidential data.

The second type of microcomputer software package for numerical analysis is the electronic spreadsheet. Many institutional researchers will purchase (and cost-justify) their first microcomputer primarily for word processing but soon discover that it is the electronic spreadsheet that has the widest and most essential applications to their work. Even the early, fairly rudimentary spreadsheet programs running on microcomputers with 64K or less of internal memory proved to be enormously useful for performing many of the tasks that are so fundamental to the institutional research and planning function. The more recent and powerful integrated programs, with their ability to integrate spreadsheet analyses with word processing, graphics, data base management, and communications, have even greater potential usefulness.

Perhaps the simplest application of electronic spreadsheets can be described as word processing for tables. Tabular reports showing numerical information arranged in rows and columns are ubiquitous in institutional research and require untold hours of staff time to prepare. One common form of such reports shows two or more sets of numbers along with the absolute and relative differences between them, for example, a table might show tuition rates for each of the past ten years, then calculate the percentage change in tuition during the most recent ten-year, five-year, two-year, and one-year periods. This type of analysis is tedious and time-consuming to prepare the first time; many an institutional researcher has come to dread the task of preparing the annual updates. Yet, with an electronic spreadsheet it is a simple matter to delete the data for the first year in the table, add the data for the current year to the tenth column or row, and have all the percentages recalculated automatically.

A more complex application of electronic spreadsheets involves the development of simple projection models that use historical trend data to predict future events. For example, projected enrollment levels at an institution are frequently based on so-called cohort survival curves, which measure (or predict) the number of students in a particular entering cohort who will enroll at the institution in each of the following five or six years. It is a simple matter to enter into an electronic spreadsheet the enrollment patterns for one or more entering cohorts. The microcomputer can then calculate the cohort survival curves and use them to project future enrollment levels. With such a model, it is possible to test a number of different what-if scenarios, for example, to test the impact on enrollment of specified changes in the size of entering cohorts or the enrollment patterns of students in them or to determine how many students should be admitted in each cohort in order to stay under a predetermined enrollment ceiling. Similar models can be used to examine the size of faculty under different assumptions about retirement or resignation rates and different hiring and promotion policies.

In some cases, institutional researchers have begun to adapt to microcomputer models containing large numbers of variables and complex interactions that were originally developed to be run on mainframe computers. For example, both Yale and Harvard University have recently converted their very large and complex budget planning models that were developed in the late 1970s under EFPM, the EDUCOM Financial Planning Model, and that run on IBM 4341 computers to models that use Lotus 1-2-3 on microcomputers. Similarly, a model of Yale's undergraduate tuition income and financial aid expenditures was converted from a mainframe to a microcomputer running SuperCalc. The input to this model was a set of aggregate statistics based on a large data set extracted from the student records system's dedicated minicomputer and calculated on a mainframe computer with SPSS. The variables in the model included such items as the percentage of students receiving financial aid, average parental contributions and student summer earnings, average travel costs, and so forth. The model was used first to calculate historical trends in each variable and then, by projecting the resulting trends into the future, to project total tuition income and financial aid expenditures under a variety of conditions (for example, under varying assumptions about the growth rate of tuition, the percentage of students receiving aid, the growth rate of parental income, and so forth).

Graphics. Norris (1983) has argued that the old saying about a picture being worth a thousand words is particularly true for institutional researchers. The audience for the planning and analytical reports produced by an office of institutional research includes some decision makers who understand and relish detailed tabular presentations (especially faculty members from the social sciences, who have made careers out of interpreting such statistical information), some who prefer graphical presentations (especially members of boards of trustees from the corporate world, where they are regularly supplied with elaborate and expensive visual displays of information), and some who prefer or demand that all findings, conclusions, and recommendations be couched in clear, concise, cogent prose. In the past, graphics were simply not practical in many offices due to the amount of time, money, and expertise that was required to produce them. Fortunately, many institutional researchers are discovering that these limitations no longer exist, and graphic displays of quantitative information are appearing with increasing frequency.

With graphics, it is possible to display a very large amount of information in a form that can be understood quickly and easily. For example, one of the critical inputs to the annual decision about tuition rates at many private institutions is information about how the growth rate of tuition in recent years compares with various measures of inflation. When these data are displayed in tabular form, they appear as long columns of numbers showing annual tuition levels for the past ten or twenty years or more alongside data about the consumer price index, the GNP implicit price deflator, median family income, per capita income, and so forth; other columns of data show the year-to-year changes in each index. It is not hard to imagine that the density of information displayed in such a table is very high, and the sheer volume of information becomes overwhelming. However, when the same information is displayed graphically, the historical trends and comparisons become immediately evident.

Telecommunications. The success of institutional research depends in large measure on its interdependence with other people, other offices, and other functions at an institution (Ridge, 1978). Therefore, of the many applications of microcomputers, the one that is potentially the most important for institutional researchers is their ability to communicate with other computer systems, including microcomputers, minicomputers, and mainframes located in the same room, in another room, building, or campus; or literally anywhere else in the world. Through telecommunications, microcomputers can be used to gain access to the processing power of other computers, to the people who use those systems, and to the information stored in them.

Two kinds of software are necessary in order for a microcomputer to become fully functional as a communications device. The first kind is called a *terminal emulation* program. As the name suggests, it allows the microcomputer to function as a remote terminal. In most institutions, terminals have become the predominant, if not the exclusive, means for accessing large multiuser computer systems, and most institutional researchers are familiar with the use of terminals for online or interactive computing. Through the use of a terminal emulation program, a microcomputer can eliminate the need for a terminal. And, if the microcomputer is portable, institutional researchers can use a terminal in the convenience of their own office, home, or elsewhere.

Terminals or microcomputers functioning as terminals are used most frequently to access local computer systems, that is, systems located at the user's own institution. Yet, through the wonders of telecommunications, data processing need no longer be limited by geographic boundaries or by the capabilities of the computers available locally. It is now possible to gain access to a computer system located across the country almost as easily and almost as cheaply as it is to one located across the hall. For example, many institutional researchers have used EFPM, EDUCOM's modeling software that runs on Cornell University's computer system and that is available through TELENET, to develop planning models for their own campuses. Others have discovered that, although a particular software package is not available on their own campus, it may be available through a network such as EDUNET. Microcomputers, when used as remote terminals on these networks, greatly expand the institutional research's arsenal of analytical tools.

Microcomputers are sometimes referred to as *intelligent workstations,* for, unlike so-called dumb terminals, they have the ability not only to send and receive information but also to store and retrieve it. Files containing data, reports, memoranda, messages, or other information can therefore be created off line on the microcomputer and later transferred to another computer through the use of a second type of communications software known as a *file transfer* program, and files stored on other computers can be transferred to a microcomputer with the same software. Since the ability to communicate effectively rests at the core of the institutional research function, any program that facilitates the flow of information can be immensely useful. The use of electronic mail is perhaps the simplest and clearest example of how microcomputers and telecommunications are gaining increasing use by institutional researchers. A more important example of the use of microcomputers for communications is the types of interinstitutional data exchange programs discussed by Bloom and Montgomery (1980). One recent example of such a program is the Higher Education Data System organized by John Dunn at Tufts University, which uses EDUNET as the network for data exchange and microcomputers running Lotus 1-2-3 as the software for preparing and organizing the data. Formal networks of institutional researchers sharing information via networked microcomputers will appear with increasing frequency.

Finally, microcomputers and telecommunications provide institutional researchers with access to a tremendous amount of information in remote data bases, such as the ERIC data bases, and the wide range of bibliographical and other information available through such public resources as The Source and DIALOG. Access to these nationally available data banks as well as to comparative information gathered from other institutions has been described by Saunders (1979) as an increasingly important tool for the institutional research analyst.

Data Management. One type of microcomputer software with a number of potential applications that has seen little actual use to date among institutional researchers is data management tools—data base managers, query languages, data dictionaries, and report generators. Institutional researchers have generally made little use of such software even on mainframe computers, for the primary responsibility for maintaining large data bases rests with the operating offices at an institution (for example, the registrar, the bursar, the admissions office, the financial aid office, and so forth) not with the institutional research office. Yet, there are several areas where the ability to create, update, and maintain a research data file, to sort and search the information that it contains, and to report it in a number of different formats may prove to be extremely useful to an institutional researcher. Perhaps the most obvious example of such an application is the institutional factbook and its annual updates. Another example is analyses and reports of highly confidential or sensitive information, where it is sometimes discomforting to maintain files or generate reports on the campus's mainframe computers. Data bases of modest size can be handled quite adequately by the integrated packages. These packages have commands for query and sort operations, distribution tables, and bivariate reports, and they will probably satisfy the overwhelming percentage of analysis and planning needs. Much larger data bases can be accommodated by specialized microcomputer packages, which then can transfer data to spreadsheet and graphics packages.

Custom Programming. Finally, institutional researchers sometimes face tasks that seem suited for microcomputers but for which no applications software is available. In such instances, it is necessary to write customized programs using one of the many languages available for microcomputers. One example is a program written in BASIC at the State University of New York's Albany campus to estimate the net price of higher education in New York state for students with different characteristics. As software packages for microcomputers become more flexible and powerful, the need for such programming will in all likelihood decrease.

Guidelines for Using Microcomputers

Perhaps the only aspect of microcomputers that exceeds their usefulness in institutional research and planning is the new or potential user's expectations about their usefulness. It is easy to understand whence such enthusiasm comes, given the ongoing media blitz about microcomputers, their pervasiveness on our campuses and in society, and the proselytizing of recent converts to microcomputing. Nevertheless, a new user's satisfaction with and successful implementation of microcomputer technology frequently demand informed decisions and realistic expectations about what microcomputers can and cannot do and how easily they can do these things. Such is the purpose of the advice and guidelines that follow.

Purchasing a Microcomputer. The decision to purchase a microcomputer is a difficult one. The choices are many, the advice is abundant but inconsistent, the benefits seem too great and the costs too small to be true (they usually are), and the uses and impact are frequently unknown or unproved. Unfortunately, microcomputer hardware and software industries are doing little to make the decision any easier, for the recent advances in microcomputer marketing seem to exceed the advances in microcomputer technology. The uncertainties should not be allowed to dissuade the new or potential purchaser, but the need for caution, for skepticism about the claims of flashy advertisements and fast-talking salespeople, and for maintaining a tight reign on one's enthusiasm and expectations must be emphasized. Here are four useful and important rules for purchasing a microcomputer:

First, do not wait until you think you know fully and precisely how you are going to use your new microcomputer or until you can clearly justify (financially or otherwise) the decision to spend scarce resources on such a comparatively new and essentially unknown technology. Microcomputers are enormously flexible, and your use will expand and diversify as your experience and knowledge increase. After all, the millions of microcomputer owners who use and swear by their systems cannot all be wrong. Potential purchasers should neither expect nor require that microcomputers immediately save money, for in fact they cost money, especially in capital investments. The advantages of microcomputers are realized over the long term, frequently in indirect ways—for example, in better information that is more readily available and more effectively communicated. As McCredie (1981) notes, the same pattern has long been evident for other types of computer systems. Despite the continuing decline in the cost of computer hardware, institutions must be prepared to make large incremental capital investments if they are to take full advantage of this new technology.

Second, do not be paralyzed by trying to look just over the horizon. You will wait forever for the technology to stabilize or for some final system to become available. There will always be a new, improved, more powerful, less expensive hardware or software system soon to be released.

Third, do not underestimate either the initial or the continuing cost of owning a microcomputer. Hardware and software costs add up quickly. Furthermore, the ongoing costs of upgrades and enhancements can be considerable but well worthwhile. Finally, recognize that it is the rare owner of a microcomputer who will be satisfied for long with his or her first system. The day you take it out of the box is the day you begin planning for your next system.

Fourth, unless you or someone on whom you can call for assistance has a great deal of expertise, experience, and time, yours should not be the only office on campus with a particular kind of system. Do not purchase the most recently introduced state-of-the-art system, even though it may appear to be more powerful and less expensive than more commonly available systems, unless you can reasonably expect that other individuals or offices will soon purchase the same system. A critical mass of users is your most important support group, for the best way to learn to use a new system or to seek solutions to your problems and answers to your questions is to ask others who have faced similar problems. The newest technology or software may appear very attractive in the magazine or showroom, but it can be very frustrating if you cannot find ready answers to the myriad of questions that inevitably arise. In short, an active user community is an essential support mechanism for new or experienced microcomputer users.

In summary, it is fortunate that a fairly conservative approach is both feasible and wise in purchasing a microcomputer. Since most systems are easy to expand, you can begin with a basic system, become familiar with its usefulness and limitations, and then add hardware and software as they are needed.

Implementing a New System. According to one television advertisement, all the new microcomputer owner needs to do is take the various components out of their boxes, plug in a few cables, and be up and operating in less than thirty seconds. Most users will find that the process of implementing a new microcomputer system requires somewhat more time and knowledge than that. This is not to deny that computer manufacturers and software developers have made enormous progress in improving the clarity of the instruction manuals and documentation that they provide and in boosting the user-friendliness of their systems. Furthermore, independent authors of both books and programs have begun to flood the market with online tutorials and well-written training manuals for all the popular hardware and software. Nevertheless, the new user should not underestimate the amount of time it will take to become comfortable and proficient in the use of a microcomputer. Also, microcomputers can be very engaging. As the old saying goes, time flies when you're having fun. There will always be new hardware or software to investigate and, if acquired, to learn. Finally, even an experienced user will encounter questions and problems that must be resolved. Many of these requests come from other, less-experienced users seeking assistance.

It is essential for all new users to have access to an experienced user who has the time, the patience, and the responsibility for hand-holding while the new user gains a moderate level of skill and comfort with the system. In some institutions, the office of institutional research has, either by design or by default, begun to perform this essential duty.

You should avoid overuse of and overreliance on microcomputers. There is some danger than institutional researchers may become the hackers of the administration, selecting or searching out tasks that can be done with the office's new technological toy.

Impact of Microcomputers. As has perhaps been obvious in what I have said here, the use of microcomputers by institutional researchers and other administrators will have far-reaching consequences, particularly for the institutional researcher.

In some instances, the institutional researcher may at first view the microcomputer as a potential threat, since many of the decision makers and departments that formerly called on institutional research for information and analytical support will use microcomputers to meet their own needs. However, this kind of change in external demands should be viewed by the institutional researcher as an opportunity rather than as a threat, for it means that he or she is now free to pursue more challenging, less mundane tasks. The situation is analogous in many ways to that of the secretary who finds that microcomputers have reduced the clerical workload.

Microcomputers and telecommunications will permit and perhaps require greater communications among different offices. Many institutional researchers will thus find themselves involved in decisions at the departmental level, whereas in the past they were involved primarily in decision making at the level of central administration. In short, microcomputers will hasten the trend toward decentralization that has been apparent on many campuses for some time.

Institutional researchers may find themselves playing an even more important leadership role in information systems design and management than they have in the past. Experience has shown that centralized administrative data processing departments have been quite resistant to the microcomputer revolution, fearing (and rightfully so) that it will threaten their power if not their very existence. On many campuses, therefore, the administrative computing experts have been reluctant to assume a leadership role in implementing microcomputer-based systems. The way is therefore open for institutional researchers to fill this void.

Conclusion

The spread of microcomputers will change the functions of institutional research once again. This new technology will gain increasing use within offices of institutional research, for it can greatly facilitate the analysis and reporting of information. Yet, microcomputers will never replace larger computer systems entirely, for there will always be a need for mass data storage, shared access, and intensive number crunching. Microcomputers should therefore be thought of not as alternatives but as complements to other types of systems. Institutional researchers must prepare for, cope with, and take fullest advantage of the new technology.

References

Bloom, A. M., and Montgomery, J. R. "Conducting Data Exchange Programs." In *The AIR Professional File*, no. 5. Tallahassee, Fla.: Association for Institutional Research, 1980.

Johnson, R. R. "Computers and Liberal Education in the Humanities and Social Sciences." *AAHE Bulletin*, 1981, *34* (2), 12-13.

McCredie, J. W. "Campus Information Processing: A New Wave." *Educational Record*, 1981, *62* (4), 6-11.

Mann, R. L. "Institutional Applications of New Information Technology." In B. S. Sheehan (Ed.), *Information Technology: Innovations and Applications*. New Directions for Institutional Research, no. 35. San Francisco: Jossey-Bass, 1982.

Norris, D. M. "Triage and the Art of Institutional Research." In *The AIR Professional File*, no. 16. Tallahassee, Fla.: Association for Institutional Research, 1983.

Ridge, J. W. "Organizing for Institutional Research." In *The AIR Professional File*, no. 1. Tallahassee, Fla.: Association for Institutional Research, 1978.

Saunders, L. E. "Dealing with Information Systems: The Institutional Researcher's Problems and Prospects." In *The AIR Professional File*, no. 2. Tallahassee, Fla.: Association for Institutional Research, 1979.

Saupe, J. L. *The Functions of Institutional Research*. Tallahassee, Fla.: Association for Institutional Research, 1981.

Zinsser, M. *Writing with a Word Processor*. New York: Harper & Row, 1983.

J. Lloyd Suttle is dean of administrative affairs and dean of student affairs at Yale College. Former director of institutional research for Yale University, he has been involved extensively with the design, implementation, and use of the computer systems for both analytical and administrative purposes, and he serves as consultant to university offices on the use of microcomputers.

With technological standards now evolving, microcomputers are less mysterious and can be effectively evaluated to meet our needs.

Microware: Hard, Soft, and Firm

Leah R. Hutten

They can sit on your lap or your desk, pack in your briefcase, accompany you to an executive meeting, or store under your seat on an airplane. They can obtain the latest stock quotations or draw a graph. First seen as hobbyist toys, microcomputers quickly took hold in the business community in the late 1970s with the invention of an ingenious tool called the *electronic spreadsheet*. Their introduction to institutions of higher education soon followed. When International Business Machines (IBM) and other large-computer manufacturers entered the microcomputer field in 1981, the microcomputer became a standard office fixture along with the telephone and the typewriter.

In most institutions, the institutional research and planning (IR&P) office has taken a lead in introducing this new technology to higher education. As the branch of an institution that gathers and analyzes data and generates reports, IR&P has always needed computational tools and text reproduction systems. It has been commonplace to find in this office a computer terminal that is linked to a large computer somewhere on campus. Data base, statistical, and financial modeling programs have had widespread use in the IR&P office for a number of years.

By the late 1970s, access to large computers had become so restricted that many universities and businesses were faced with a critical shortage of computing resources: Computer systems were oversubscribed, often inaccessible, and unable to meet user needs such as word processing, spreadsheet modeling, and graphics. Large computer systems, which had changed the nature of the work environment, were not fulfilling the expectations they had helped to create. With its inexpensive price tag and versatile capabilities, the microcomputer now offers an ideal alternative.

Microcomputers are used for office clerical tasks, management decision making, and conventional tasks previously accomplished on large computers. A microcomputer can act as a terminal to a remote computer, yet it can also hold programs and data independently, and it offers new capabilities, such as graphics. Microcomputers have changed the way people work and how they work together. They have also created an amazingly prolific although sometimes confusing market situation. With 150 microcomputer manufacturers worldwide, a new vocabulary to untangle, and often contradictory and misleading advice from salespersons, there is a clear need to unravel the mysteries surrounding microcomputers. This chapter offers a basic introduction to microcomputer systems and the information needed for making intelligent purchasing decisions.

Because a microcomputer system can be an expensive acquisition for a small office, the purchase decision needs to be made carefully. The first step is to evaluate the data and word processing needs of the office. It is helpful to consider both current needs and needs four to five years hence and to obtain consultation from technology specialists. Five years ago, when few people realized the potential of word processing, industry experts correctly predicted its impact. In seeking vendors' opinions, however, keep in mind that salespersons are trained to convince you that your needs are great.

Next, determine which needs are being met with existing data processing capabilities and review the additional benefits that microcomputer systems would provide; some typical expected benefits are increased productivity, more timely reporting, and more effective use of staff time. If a needs analysis indicates that a microcomputer system is indeed justified, then it becomes necessary to select a few systems for evaluation.

A visit to local computer stores is a good way to start gathering information. You may also be able to contact manufacturers' representatives on your campus. Products are often compared in consumer-oriented computer publications. Questions not answered by salespersons and publications can be addressed directly to product vendors. Once the relevant facts have been collected, a cost-benefit comparison among systems should be made; many universities require one.

The computer industry uses the term *hardware* to refer to machinery or equipment and the term *software* to refer to computer programs and applications. Since prominent hardware and software systems seem to change in the marketplace every six months, no specific products are recommended here. Rather, I focus on information and guidelines that will be useful for evaluating any available hardware and software products.

Hardware

Although the complete microcomputer is approximately the size of a typewriter, the microprocessor—the engine or heart of the computer—is only one-quarter-inch square. The miniaturization of computers from the huge machines of the 1960s is a direct result of the development of transistors in 1948 and of integrated circuit technology in 1961. A microcomputer system is composed of the microprocessor or central processing unit (CPU); a memory; a power supply; and various peripheral devices, such as a keyboard, video screen, and disk drives used for storage and communication.

The Microprocessor. While there are hundreds of different brands of microcomputers, most manufacturers use the same basic microprocessor chips, and thus the number of true variants is limited to less than a dozen. These are classified by the number of bits (binary digits) in their internal architecture. The number of bits in the microcomputer character, which is also known as a *byte,* governs speed, storage capacity, and precision with large numbers. The first microcomputers used eight-bit microprocessors, but production of microcomputer systems now takes advantage of very large-scale integration, which you will often encounter as the acronym VSLI, which enables manufacturers to employ sixteen- and thirty-two-bit microprocessors in their designs.

As an illustration of how microprocessors differ, consider that the typical eight-bit microprocessor can manage 65,525 characters of memory; in computer jargon, we call this a *64K* microcomputer, where *K* is a shorthand abbreviation of 2^{10} (that is, 1,024). A sixteen-bit processor allows the execution of more sophisticated programs. Generally speaking, the more user-friendly a program is, the larger and more complicated it becomes. Some microcomputers now contain two microprocessors—one eight-bit and one sixteen-bit, two sixteen-bit, or one sixteen-bit and one thirty-two-bit—to increase their capability and power.

Memory and Storage. The primary power of the computer rests in its ability to repeat simple tasks any number of times. A computer program is a set of instructions in some computer language that defines repetitive tasks to the computer. Programs and data are normally stored on some external media and then loaded into memory for execution. The central processing unit fetches computer steps from memory and executes them in sequence.

Microcomputers have two forms of memory: random access memory (RAM) and read-only memory (ROM). An advertisement specifying that a computer has 64K of memory usually refers to RAM, which can be used for specific applications. It is a misconception, however, that a 64K microcomputer can store 64,000 letters or numbers. A large section of RAM is reserved for system software and programs needed to make the computer function; only the remainder can be used to store data. Large numbers must be reconstructed with logarithms and stored in contiguous memory locations. Thus, an eight-bit microcomputer with 64K of RAM can store about 13,000 numbers in RAM. RAM is a volatile form of memory; that is, its contents disappear when the computer is turned off.

ROM contains the operating system and specific language interpreters, it is nonvolatile, and its contents cannot be altered by the user. A device such as a ROM chip, which incorporates programs into hardware, is often referred to as *firmware*. With firmware, programs execute faster and need not be reloaded into the computer every time they are needed. Recently designed computer systems contain extensive applications of programs in firmware.

External storage devices having magnetic properties retain information when the computer is off. These devices include floppy and hard disks, bubbles, and cassette tape. Laser devices are also used for information storage, but, unlike magnetic devices, they cannot be altered or updated.

The most common storage medium for microcomputers is the floppy disk. The floppy disk, which is made of plastic coated with metal oxide, is manufactured in a number of sizes, but the five-and-one-quarter-inch diameter diskette has been a microcomputer standard for the last few years. Some of the newer microcomputers are now using three-and-one-half-inch diameter disks enclosed in hard plastic protective cases. These disks have equal or greater capacity and are another example of increasing minaturization in the industry.

Information is recorded on the magnetic surface of the diskette in concentric circles called *tracks*. Floppy disks are classified not only by the diameter but by the number of usable recording sides and memory density. Double-sided double-density (DS/DD) diskettes hold four times the amount of information contained on single-sided single-density (SS/SD) diskettes. A five-and-one-quarter-inch DS/DD diskette typically has a capacity of 360K bytes (approximately fifty pages of standard typewritten text), while an eight-inch diskette has a capacity of more than a million bytes. Computer programs are purchased on diskettes, and additional diskettes are needed for storing documents, data sets, and computer programs created by the user. The diskette is read from a disk drive that is usually part of the microcomputer system. Most computer applications require two disk drives: one for programs, one for data.

Diskettes and drives need to be given the same care as cassette tapes and recorders. Disk heads need to be cleaned periodically, and copies—called *backups*—should be made for important diskettes. Diskette recording quality diminishes with age, use, and exposure to the environment, so it is desirable to purchase only high-quality diskettes that are certified to be error-free on both sides.

While floppy diskettes are compact and easy to transport, the hard disk, popularly called a Winchester disk, improves on the speed, capacity, and accuracy of the floppy. A five-and-one-quarter-inch Winchester disk can store more than five million characters (five megabytes) of information, it can be accessed at ten times the speed of a floppy diskette, and it is considered to be essentially error-free. These features are made possible because the disk is sealed from the environment. A Winchester disk drive is usually installed in as well so that software can be read into the system. A hard disk system is ideal for users with large data base requirements, but it adds a thousand dollars or more the the system's price, and most lack backup capability for larger files.

Magnetic tapes are not often used with small business computers because tape drives are imprecise and transfer information very slowly. Unlike the random access of disks, information on tapes must be accessed in sequential order. Magnetic tape cassettes are a primary storage device for home computers, however, because of their low cost.

The advantage of bubble memory (so named because of its shape) lies in its compactness and nonvolatility, but bubble memory is expensive, it is low in capacity, and it has had limited field testing. Information is stored in the bubble on a grid of magnetic flakes embedded in silicon. Bubbles are manufactured in 64K to 512K modules and often found in expensive portable computers.

What has become known as the electronic disk is a battery-powered complementary-metal-oxide-semiconductor (CMOS) memory. In addition to its nonvolatility, CMOS memory has the advantages of speed, price, and capacity (up to one megabyte). It can be used to extend RAM or as an electronic form of disk storage, speeding access to software and data a hundredfold. Like many extra features, it consumes one or more of the expansion slots in the computer and thus limits future expansion for other peripherals.

Laser recording, familiar from the entertainment industry, is also used for storing computer information. At present, optically recorded media are *read-only,* but erasable laser recording devices are nearing production. With laser techniques, millions of pieces of information can be recorded on a strip about the size of the magnetic bar on a credit card. Retrieval rates from optically recorded media are exceptionally fast.

It is useful to achieve a balance between the amount of extended storage capacity in a system and the amount of internal memory. Abundant external storage is needed for data bases with more than a few hundred entries, while sufficient internal RAM memory is needed for spreadsheet analysis, statistics, and other intensive numerical processing.

Devices that permit transmission of instructions or data to the microcomputer and retrieval of the results constitute an interface between human and machine. The process of sending information to the computer is called *input.* Direct interface between two or more computers is termed *networking.*

Input Devices

Keyboard. Not long ago in the evolution of information technology, the primary input and output medium for computers was the punched card. In today's computers, most input originates at the keyboard. A keyboard can be built-in, or it can be separate, so that it can be placed to the side of the console or even on one's lap. Detachable keyboards are connected to the computer by cable or by infrared light wave transmission.

A keyboard requires specific features to accomplish word and data processing. A numeric keypad is needed for data entry, directional arrows are needed for cursor positioning, upper and lower case are needed for word processing, and special control keys (CONTROL, BACKSPACE, ESCAPE) are required for communications with mainframe computers. Special function keys are helpful as they allow greater program flexibility, and touch and positioning of keys that resemble those on a standard typewriter keyboard are desirable for user comfort.

Mouse. A small unit called a *mouse* is an important input device designed for systems that employ screen graphics and menu-driven software. Movement of the mouse on the tabletop translates into cursor positions on the screen. A mouse has one or more input buttons as well for choosing preset program options. Some users feel that the frequent need to switch hands back and forth from the mouse to the keyboard for inputting words and numbers is a distinct disadvantage. Also, most mouse controllers require a fair amount of tabletop space for movement.

Digitizer. In general, devices that translate spatial coordinates into computerized information are referred to as *digitizers*. Although less commonly used in office system environments, these devices make the use of computers much easier. In addition to the mouse, digitizing devices include graphics tablets, light pens, touch-sensitive screens, and devices that digitize video and audio information. Bar code readers like those in the supermarket, mark sense readers, card readers, and other devices traditionally used for input to large computers are also available for microcomputers. In future years, we can expect to witness major improvements in voice input systems.

Output Devices

Monitor. The monitor, also referred to as the *display, screen, terminal,* or *cathode ray tube* (CRT), is the primary microcomputer output device. A monitor has the same picture tube as a television set, but it does not receive television channel broadcasts. Rather, it is directly connected to the computer by a special video cable. Monitor screens range in size from five inches to about seventeen inches in diagonal measurement, and they are also made as wall-size projection devices. They are available in monochrome—usually green, white, or amber on black—or in full color, which is useful not only for graphics but also for highlighting the special effects available in some programs.

An image on a monitor is normally produced by illuminating phosphor-coated dots called *pixels* by a method known as *raster scan.* A close view will verify that the image is actually a pattern of dots. Screen resolutions can vary from 260 pixels horizontally and 300 pixels vertically to more than 1,000 pixels in each dimension. A high-quality monitor can display at least

600 by 400 pixels. The resolution itself depends on the number of pixels, the pixel width or pitch, the distance between pixels, the display memory, the scanning speed, and the speed with which the screen accepts data from the computer. A monitor with good resolution reduces eyestrain because it produces a sharper picture. Precise focus and antiglare features are important for all monitors, while accurate hue, tint, and contrast are essential for color displays. For color, three times as many pixels are required as for monochrome. A typical monitor displays twenty-four to twenty-five lines of eighty to one-hundred-fifty characters of text. This is in contrast to low-quality broadcast television receivers, which typically can display only forty readable characters per line.

Another type of monitor is often used in high-quality dedicated word processing and graphics systems. A vector rather than a raster scan technique is used to produce a crystal clear image. Although these monitors are easier on the eyes, they are considerably more expensive due to the complexity of their electronic components.

The liquid crystal display (LCD), familiar in digital watches and calculators, has gained considerable acceptance as an output display device, especially for small portable computers, because of its low cost and light weight. Larger LCD displays have twenty-five lines of eighty characters and can be used for low-resolution graphics in average room light conditions.

The flat screen monitor, which can use LCD technology and other advanced methods, has been greatly improved by Japanese electronics manufacturers. Flat black-and-white screens have been available for a number of years in high-priced portable computers, but color displays, presently used only in television sets, should be available for computers in a few years. The flat screen display makes computer systems more compact, significantly lighter, and very portable.

Printer. The importance of the printed word has not been lost in the electronic information age. The printer is the standard hard copy output device. The high-speed dot matrix printer is used for draft copies of text, program listings, and graphics. The slower letter-quality printer is used for important documents and word processing.

Inexpensive dot matrix printers use impact, thermal, photographic, and ink jet technologies. The more expensive dot matrix laser printer, primarily used with larger computer systems, has extraordinary speed and quality. Some of the graphics-oriented dot matrix printers use a three-color ribbon for multicolor graphics. Early dot matrix printers formed characters from a seven- by nine-dot grid, but a quality dot matrix printer today uses a seventeen- by nineteen-dot grid, and the resulting print is almost letter-quality. True letter-quality printers are more expensive than most dot matrix printers, and their print speeds range from ten to sixty characters per second (CPS), in contrast to the one-hundred-twenty CPS of the dot matrix printer. The daisywheel, an impact device, is the primary technology used in letter-quality printers.

To be useful, a printer needs to be supported by all the software systems that you purchase. Printing speed, which increases with price, is the next most important factor to be evaluated. A letter-quality printer obtained for word processing applications should print 132 characters per line and offer a selection of fonts and pitches, proportional spacing, bidirectional printing, underline, boldface, and tab indentations. For other applications, either a dot matrix or letter-quality printer can be used. Consider future needs as well as budget constraints when selecting a printer.

Plotter. Hard copy graphics devices are another standard computer peripheral. These devices recreate permanent copy of the screen image through a number of processes, including plotting, photocopying, photography, and printing. A pen plotter produces the highest-quality graphics on paper or transparencies. Pen plotters are manufactured in drum or flatbed varieties and come equipped with one or more colored pens. A quality pen plotter has a 10,000- by 10,000-point resolution and costs under $1,000. A photographic attachment allows the creation of snapshots and slides directly from the screen or indirectly from memory. For direct screen photography, a plug-in graphics board can be used to enhance the screen image. Graphics made on a printer lack the sharpness of other hard copy media, since they use dot patterns.

Modem. While microcomputers have been primarily designed as stand-alone desktop computers, they often serve as terminals to other remote computers, either mainframes or other microcomputers. The modem is an essential component for telecommunications and network access. A modem translates electronic signals into sound frequencies and connects a computer to a telephone outlet, thus providing access to other computers via standard telephone lines. A quality modem transmits information at 1,200 baud (approximately 120 characters per second), it has both send and receive capability, and it filters extraneous noise. Some recent computer designs include a built-in modem.

A Typical System Configuration. A microcomputer with two disk drives, a flatbed plotter, a dot matrix printer, and a 1,200 baud modem is a typical configuration. The price of such a system in 1983 was about $7,000, including software; in 1984, the price had dropped to under $4,000. A letter-quality printer or a hard disk drive would each add $1,000 to this price. A quality office system usually has a parallel (or Centronics) connection for a printer and two serial connections for plotters, modems, or other devices. A good office microcomputer should be able to be upgraded to 512K of RAM and have expansion slots for future additions of memory or peripheral devices.

Portable Computers. The portable computer is fast becoming the most important personal productivity tool available today. For the first time, information processing power can accompany a busy professional to a board meeting or vacation retreat. Designed as self-contained computers and communications devices, the best portables have flat screens, bubble memory, battery power, and built-in modems, and they are sufficiently small that they can fit into a briefcase. A portable computer provides the capability of working at home or during travel as well as of presenting information at meetings outside the office. A quarter of the microcomputers produced in 1983 were designed to be portable.

Compatible Computers. In the past few years, some computer industry giants have become front-runners in the personal computer marketplace. Many new companies and some existing companies that have redesigned their systems are now offering products that they claim to be compatible with those of the market leaders. This recent manufacture of compatibles has resulted in unexpected standards in the microcomputer industry: The characteristics of the copied machines have become de facto standards. Compatibles offer considerable cost savings, but despite sales and advertising claims, they tend to lack full compatibility with the copied systems. Less than 100 percent compatibility means that some programs will not execute. To assess compatibility, it is wise to talk with other consumers or watch the intended programs and peripherals actually work on the machine being considered.

Software

As already noted, the term *hardware* refers to computer equipment, while the term *software* refers to operating systems, programming languages, and applications programs. Although the appearance of hard drives and programmed chips is reducing the differences between hardware and software, the distinction is still common and significant within the computer industry.

Operating Systems. The operating system is the software interface between the user and the microprocessor. A good operating system is easy to use ("friendly"), and it offers powerful input-output control, storage management, and other utilities and functions. Some operating systems are proprietary and run only on one manufacturer's equipment; others are generic and transportable between different microcomputers. Although generic operating systems allow standard computer programs to run on different microcomputers, they are often tailored to special hardware features of a particular computer brand.

CP/M, which stands for the words *control program/microcomputers,* is considered the standard operating system for most eight-bit microcomputers, and it runs nearly 2,000 applications. Two rival operating systems available for sixteen-bit microcomputers are CP/M–86, an extension of CP/M, and MS-DOS, which stands for the words *Microsoft disc-operating system.* Because MS–DOS was selected as the standard operating system for the IBM Personal Computer, there is more applications software now under development for it than for other systems. UNIX, a powerful operating system popular on minicomputers and well liked by programmers, has been used in thirty-two-bit microcomputers, and a sixteen-bit version is now under development. Some industry representatives believe that UNIX will become the future standard operating system for all microcomputers.

In addition to these single-user single-task operating systems, multiuser multitask operating systems are also available. Multiuser operating systems allow a single microprocessor to be shared by four to eight workstations. A multitask operating system allows printing or plotting during execution of other tasks. The combination of both features in one operating system provides capabilities similar to those found on large mainframe computers.

Programming Languages. There are more than twenty-five computer programming languages in use today. While these are of little concern to most users, since applications programs (prewritten programs) are purchased with the microcomputer, an understanding of programming can enhance one's appreciation for computers. Also, knowledge of programming can be useful for expanding a system's capabilities. Microcomputers usually have a BASIC language interpreter installed in ROM. Pascal, FORTRAN, C, COBOL, Assembler, and other languages are available for most small business systems. Computer language compilers, which translate commands into machine language, are often packaged with other introductory software products, or they can be purchased for around $200.

Applications Programs. Of the many tasks accomplished by microcomputers, six are of special interest to institutional research and planning offices: word processing, spreadsheets, statistics, graphics, data base management, and communications. The primary features to evaluate in all applications software programs are these: ease of use, quality of documentation, integration, and support of hardware devices. Programs with menus (lists of alternative choices) are easier to learn and use then programs that use command languages. Graphics-oriented microcomputers employ graphic menus that contain a set of small figures called *icons* instead of English words and phrases. Good software will usually display usage hints on the screen and permit additional help to be obtained at the touch of a key. Documentation should be easy to understand and contain examples and sample sessions. Integration refers to the capability for transferring files and data quickly and easily from one application to another. For example, a table created with a spreadsheet should be accessible for editing with a word processing package or for graphic display. Integrated software systems that simultaneously display data, graphs, and texts by means of windows offer the most power. Finally, applications software should support printers, plotters, and other hardware devices.

Word Processing. Word processing (WP) is considered a development equal in importance to the printing press. WP is ideal for producing articles, reports, letters, and extensive mail lists. It provides electronic recording of information, updating capability, and processing of personalized form letters, and it even offers spelling verification and sorting functions.

The first step in selecting a WP system is to evaluate the types of documents normally produced in your office environment. Determine the need for footnoting, title centering, indexing, underlining, boldface, and superscript and subscript capability and the frequency of personalized mailings and updates or revisions. Different word processing systems are appropriate for different purposes; some are best for scholarly articles, others for business reports. When selecting among systems, take time to study the manual and try a sample session. In contrast to dedicated word processing systems, microcomputer WP systems have compromised between the desirable characteristics of program power and ease of use. WP packages that are powerful tend to be difficult to learn and awkward to use; the WP packages that are easy to learn tend to have more limited functions.

Spreadsheets. Planners are well aware of the time consumed in preparing budget or other numerical projections. Spreadsheet programs are designed as an electronic representation of the familiar handwritten budget spreadsheet. Any entry on the sheet can be a label, number, or formula. Row and column operations can be performed, but the real power of the electronic spreadsheet is that, as figures in one entry change, the spreadsheet automatically updates all other dependent entries. A spreadsheet format allows users to ask what-if questions and to obtain instant projections. The spreadsheet is an ideal tool for modeling activities of any sort in research and planning offices.

An electronic spreadsheet needs to be large enough to accomplish specific applications; 256 columns by 1,000 rows are recommended. The full capacity of a spreadsheet can be realized only if the computer system has the appropriate memory support, usually a minimum of 256K. Spreadsheet data should be easy to transfer to graphics and data base systems.

Statistics. IR&P offices tend to generate lots of numbers. While the power and flexibility of the statistical analysis packages available on large computers are still needed for major studies, microcomputers offer a valuable tool for smaller studies. The range of statistics available is limited, but better programs are now being developed, including miniversions of particular mainframe programs.

Microcomputer statistics packages usually limit the number of observations and variables that can be analyzed, but some have dynamic memory allocation that uses all installed RAM memory. Statistical analysis on a microcomputer is slower than it is on large computers unless a specialized numerical coprocessor is installed. It is advisable to verify the precision and accuracy of a microcomputer statistics package with data published by the American Statistical Association or data previously analyzed with a mainframe statistics package. Also, when selecting a statistics package, it is wise to review the table of contents, to determine limitations on the size of the data matrix, and to find out how much memory is required.

Graphics. Microcomputers offer outstanding graphics capabilities. Pictures including bar charts, pie charts, line graphs, and flow charts can instantly be created on the screen and then transferred to hard copy media, graphic presentations, annual reports, and other planning documents. The microcomputer graphics field was spurred on by computer-aided design (CAD) and computer-aided manufacturing (CAM), but important applications are now available in business graphics.

Analytical graphics, usually linked to a spreadsheet, produce simple graphs that can easily be revised as numbers are updated. Since analytical graphics are primarily designed to support numerical analysis, they have limited options and design features. They can be refined with a presentation graphics package to produce high-quality photo-ready graphics. A good menu-driven graphics package provides ten to twenty optional graphic formats, choice of fonts, and sizes of text and the capability of combining pictures with text. While somewhat less easy to learn, command-oriented graphics software is much more flexible.

A plotter or other hard copy device is needed to make permanent copies of graphics. The software manual indicates the specific plotters that are supported. Be sure that the graphics package you select has a simple interface for transferring data from data base, statistical, and spreadsheet systems. Because graphics software is hardware-dependent, most packages run on only one system. This may limit your hardware choice.

Data Base Systems. A data base can be used to store names and addresses of alumni, the student information system, personnel files, and many other types of records. A data base provides an electronic filing cabinet for the office. With the availability of hard disk storage, microcomputer data base capacity has been greatly improved, although microcomputers cannot yet rival the speed and capacity of large mainframe computers.

A data base system should have a good screen formatter, a flexible report generator, and dynamic searching and sorting features. A careful review of the data base manual is needed to determine whether the capacity meets your data base needs, whether the software supports a hard disk system or not. A command-driven data base management program can be customized to specific applications with the assistance of a programmer, but menu-driven systems are simpler to use. As with other software, it is important to read all documentation before purchasing a package and to apply the system to sample problems.

Communications. In addition to being a stand-alone computer, the microcomputer can serve as a communications link with other computers. The advantage that a microcomputer has over simple terminals is that it can transfer files to its disk system for future processing.

Ideally, communication software requires little user knowledge. It is capable of "talking" with the host computer's operating system, of transferring files in either direction, of checking for transmission errors, and of correcting them. Unfortunately, communication protocols (formats) are complex, and most communications packages are not easy to understand. Communication is accomplished by emulating a known protocol, for example 3270 for IBM systems or VT100 for Digital Equipment Corporation mainframes. Some sophistication is needed to perform screen editing, graphics, file transfer, and other functions on the host computer.

Additional Factors Related to Microcomputer Purchases

So far, important features in microcomputer hardware and software have been discussed. However, some additional points should be considered in purchasing a microcomputer. For example, the quick pace of technology has resulted in a very short life cycle for microcomputers. With good planning, obsolescence can be avoided. Select only those systems that are designed to be easily upgraded, expanded, or integrated into future systems produced by the same manufacturer. Seek equipment that is durable and designed with user comfort and safety in mind. Because of rapid transition within the industry, it is wise to purchase systems from companies that have a reputation for quality and service, despite the added cost.

Many universities have group purchasing plans that offer discounts ranging between 30 and 50 percent. If you choose a system designated by your university's computer department, it will often be compatible with central mainframes and other computers on campus, and there will be a knowledgeable user community to help you solve problems.

With the microcomputer system, you will need to purchase supplies, software, and possibly insurance, security devices, and maintenance contracts. The supplies required include paper, diskettes, and ribbons and wheels for printers. Approximately $500 to $750 needs to be budgeted annually for supplies. The same amount should be reserved for purchases of software and additional hardware, such as extra memory or graphics boards. You may need to extend university insurance policies to cover microcomputer systems in the office as well as during travel. You may also need to invest in antitheft devices specially made for computer hardware. These can add $500 to the purchase price of your computer system. Computer equipment is normally covered by warranty for only ninety days. The cost of hourly maintenance—$60 to $100 per hour—justifies the purchase of an extended maintenance contract. Maintenance contracts are offered as mail, drop-off, and on-site and priced accordingly—between 10 and 14 percent of the equipment's list price.

Space requirements, environmental factors, power requirements, and location of communication lines must be considered when a microcomputer is installed in an office. A microcomputer workstation needs about three by six feet of space. The space needs to be well-lighted and to be reasonably private and comfortable. Quality furniture that meets these requirements can add $1,000 to the system's price. Printers can be very noisy, and your printer may need either a sound hood or to be positioned where it does not disturb other staff. Humidity and temperature controls may be needed, since excessive dampness, dryness, heat, or cold can damage microcomputer equipment. Check the manuals for each piece of equipment to determine combined power requirements. The use of a power filter that prevents damage to the equipment from power failures or abrupt changes in voltage is advised. A microcomputer used for communications needs to be located near a telephone outlet.

A microcomputer system can increase personal productivity and therefore change the way people work together. It is helpful to consider in advance the impact of the microcomputer on staff responsibilities and interrelationships among office personnel. You need to decide who will be trained and how training will be provided. Some universities offer microcomputer training, but others need to find outside training programs. Staff who upgrade skills may request changes in their job levels and expect commensurate salary increases as well.

Afterword

This chapter has offered some essential facts about microcomputers and described features that are most beneficial. I hope that the information is still current when the volume goes to press. Nevertheless, it is wise to seek timely information from computer journals designed for nontechnical audiences and from computer user groups. User groups are an excellent source for demonstrations, sample program disks, newsletters, and contact with other users.

Leah R. Hutten is director of analytic studies at Tufts University, where she also has responsibility for computer literacy training programs. She has been involved in computing since 1968.

This is an era of technological marvels. Consider the microfiche and the silicon chip. In fact, the 1980s may become known as the "fiche and chip" decade.

Using Microcomputers for Distributed Information Processing

Derek M. Jamieson
Kenneth H. MacKay

It is unlikely that we can accurately forecast how we will be using computers and related technologies in the next few years. Rapid improvement in the technologies combined with dramatic reductions in cost will lead to the development of innovative applications. The use of computers to expedite communications has begun, but we suspect that it will grow apace in the next period. However, there are strong countervailing influences. Communicating is a people-oriented activity, and people resist change. In addition, the terms that we use to describe some of the new techniques are very backward-looking. *Electronic mail* emphasizes the metaphor of filing cabinets bulging with printed letters. *Computer conferencing* suggests printed proceedings and authorship of new scientific papers. Both metaphors are only approximately correct. Electronic mail is an asynchronous conversation, primarily between two individuals, that largely replaces traditional telephone conversations. Computer conferencing is an asynchronous conversation among many individuals that serves to replace committee meetings. Some new terms would be most welcome; remember the *wireless* and the *horseless carriage?*

Microcomputers contribute to communications in both direct and indirect ways—direct in the sense that micros can be used to expedite word processing, electronic messages, and other forms of electronic communication, indirect in the sense that managers and researchers can use them to prepare analyses, graphs, and summaries. Thus, the term *communication* is being used in the broad context throughout this chapter.

In the first section, we deal with the application of micro to the word processors and with word processing software on a mainframe. The second section concerns the use of commercially available software and locally developed software as an aid in decision making. The third section discusses electronic spreadsheets. In the fourth section, we show how microcomputers can function as intelligent terminals, permitting asynchronous conversations. The following section deals with the use of microcomputers in computer conferencing systems, in which micros function as intelligent terminals with local editing and filing capabilities to allow asynchronous conversations among many participants. Next, we deal with the use of micros as departmental workstations, where the micro functions both as an independent unit for local record keeping and information processing and as part of a network providing for electronic transmission of transactions, such as requisitions and purchase orders. In the following section, we consider how local area networks can be optimized with a number of micros. The concluding section outlines the issues that need to be addressed if micros are to be successfully acquired and integrated into a working organization.

Word Processing

Microprocessors may replace the dedicated word processor in more and more applications. Perhaps the best way to think of the word processor is that it is a microcomputer with some of its multifunctions removed so that the text processing function can be made as simple and easy to use as possible. The prototypical word processor comes with a good-quality screen, a keypad that is as close as possible to the layout on a typewriter, and easy connections to printers. At the low end of the word processing scale, a single processor station is connected to a printer; at the high end of the scale, several word processors share a printer.

One of the problems with word processing in the university environment lies in the training process. Usually, intensive training is given to new operators of a dedicated word processor. This training is supplied by the manufacturer of the equipment as part of the purchase price. After this training, which usually takes place over a three-day period, the trainees return to their department as "experts." However, not only may these individuals have had problems absorbing all the information thrown at them in three days, in most institutions they may also be isolated in departments without access to fellow sufferers who can exchange information and help to solidify the knowledge gained. In the rare instances where there is a large number of processors and operators, there is the possibility that individuals can assist one another and form a pool of expertise. Such situations are much more common in business than in academic or administrative departments in the average-sized university. While this training problem can occur regardless of the equipment used, it is probably less severe in the case of a general-purpose micro coupled with a text processing package than it is in the case of a dedicated word processor.

Training in the use of word processing packages on a microcomputer can also entail much time and effort. However, many individuals in the typical academic department—secretaries, clerks, researchers, and department chairmen—have begun to use micros and the word processing facility. In such a situation, the critical mass of knowledge builds up quickly, and the collective comfort level within the department aids greatly in the integration of the new technology. In contrast, dedicated word processors are of less interest to researchers and chairmen. As a result, secretaries and typists may find themselves isolated with the dedicated word processor.

There is no question that a fully equipped word processor is a very good device for producing text and reports easily, quickly, and with high-quality printing. In many situations where typed reports are a large part of the work load, the dedicated word processor is a good choice. The decision to choose a general-purpose microcomputer instead of a word processor depends on other needs in the department: electronic messaging, spreadsheet-type computations, research computing, and so on. Last but not least, cost of the two approaches to word processing differs substantially, with the general-purpose microcomputer being considerably less expensive than the dedicated word processor.

New and improved word processing packages for microcomputers continue to be announced, and some recent offerings provide facilities remarkably similar to those available on the well-established dedicated word processors. Finally, the recent announcement by a major manufacturer that the software for its dedicated word processor will be made available on its microcomputer suggests that, at least for that manufacturer, the days of the dedicated word processor are numbered.

The comparison is somewhat different between microcomputers used as text processors and remote terminals tied to a mainframe computer that use a typical text editing program. One of the minor annoyances of using a terminal connected to a mainframe is that one works with a line at a time, and one is always conscious of the transmission back and forth to the mainframe. With a microprocessor, one feels more in control of the total operation. In addition, with a microprocessor it is often the case that what you see is what you get; that is, changes that you make in your text appear immediately on the screen before you so that you are always aware of how the finished product will look. This contrasts with text processing on a mainframe computer, where the effects of a number of functional commands built into the program appear only when you produce a formatted copy.

It is probably fair to say that the command sequences are as complicated on a micro as they are on a terminal, perhaps even more so. However, the complexity varies considerably, depending on the configuration of software and hardware being used. Pairing particular software for text processing with a particular micro is important, since the command structure should be keypad-oriented. Thus, the best software is that which has incorporated many of the functions of the micro's keypad. A text processing program that does not take full advantage of the micro's flexibility is less desirable.

Another fact of which one should be aware is that some programs used for text processing are more suitable for a conventional business letter, whereas others are more suitable for scientific text. Furthermore, a number of the features that one becomes accustomed to on the mainframe, such as spelling checks, mailing list capabilities, and automatic footnoting, are available on micros only as add-ons to the basic text processing package.

Some micro text processors permit boiler plating—the use of standard paragraphs with custom insertions—but not all do. Normally, this feature is available on a mainframe. As to connecting a micro to a high-quality printer, which is done conventionally when a terminal is attached to a mainframe, this depends very much on the choice of micro and the choice of software. In some instances, a custom program written for an individual installation and its micro may be required.

Finally, word processors are often used for computerized phototypesetting. This is easy to arrange when a terminal is attached to a mainframe, but if a micro is being used, it will probably be necessary to send the information to a typesetter through the mainframe. In the event that the typesetter had the same micro as the originator of the material, then it may be possible to transfer the information on a diskette.

Decision Support Systems

Decision support systems (DSS) may be a new buzzword, but it represents an important class of computerized systems that evolved from the monolithic management information system (MIS) of the 1970s. Many definitions of the term DSS exist, but we want to consider a class of computerized aids that offer personalized facilities that can be used to help an executive or manager make decisions or process routine work. There are many packages available for micros that address the DSS area. Typically, these packages cover financial applications and allow the manager to prepare a financial model of the organization under study. After a satisfactory and reasonably accurate model has been created, it is possible to conduct many what-if studies very quickly.

Computer programming languages, such as BASIC and APL, can be used on a mainframe, minicomputer, or microcomputer to create decision support systems. Alternatively, managers themselves can set up and use electronic spreadsheets to create a DSS. However, one must consider the need to access the central data bases and to communicate with other offices. Choice of language or facility to create a DSS involves some consideration of all the interconnections to other offices and other sources of data within the institution. A decision in this regard that isolates the office of institutional research from other offices in the institution would inevitably be wrong. Downloading from the central data bases will be important, and it may even be essential in some cases.

Decision support systems can take many forms and use many different types of computing facilities. For example, some chief executive officers (CEOs) use a personalized DSS to track planning projects and management issues as they are processed through the organization. By using such a tracking facility, CEOs can detect the issues that are likely to percolate to the top at the same time. The DSS can also provide warnings that certain projects are falling behind schedule and may require special attention. Similarly, the financial analyst responsible for monitoring cash flow and investment portfolios can use a very specific DSS to aid in the prediction of cash flow and to assist in the management of investments.

Electronic Spreadsheets

A number of commercial programs are available to provide a spreadsheet capability, and the most advanced packages provide an integrated graphics capability. As with word processing, it is very important to match the software with the specific hardware.

One of the important features of electronic spreadsheet packages is a tutorial that helps the new user to become familiar with the package. The potential buyer should check the richness and completeness of the help feature in the package. Some packages provide the equivalent of two or three hundred pages of help messages, whereas others have only two or three pages. Another desirable feature for an electronic spreadsheet is the ability to expand or decrease the size of individual columns in the spreadsheet. Finally, you should check to see whether the program uses the keyboard keys as they were intended and whether it lets you see changes in format as they are being mode. The actual use of a spreadsheet package does not require any computer programming skill. It does require an appreciation of the spreadsheet concept and some knowledge of the commands available in the program.

One final caution is in order: If the naive user goes to a centralized computing center to ask for advice on electronic spreadsheet packages, he or she is likely to get a lukewarm response. In general, the computing expert is likely to look on the spreadsheet as trivial and a poor use of computing power. In marked contrast, the manager or accountant is accustomed to analyses employing spreadsheets and envisions considerable benefits resulting from an electronic version.

Electronic Message Systems

Electronic message systems (EMSs) have come into widespread use in recent years. These systems represent an electronic conversation between two individuals, and they have the facility to copy specific messages to additional individuals. The major advantage of an EMS is the ability to conduct an asynchronous conversation, thus reducing the time-wasting problems of telephone tag. Micros can be used as dumb terminals or as intelligent terminals to interface with the EMS. When the micro is used as an intelligent terminal, it can copy all messages from the host computer. The user can then read the messages at leisure and use the micro to prepare new messages that he or she transmits back to the central computer.

In addition to local electronic message systems within an organization or institution, work has begun on ways of connecting different systems. Many mail networks are under development. They bear such names as MAILNET, EDUMAIL, and E-MAIL. As one might expect, there is a great need to develop standards for electronic addresses, and these standards are currently in an early stage of evolution. Finally, commercial service bureaus and common carriers are offering public electronic message systems with various features, such as filing capabilities, keyword search, and personal calendars.

Electronic Computer Conferencing

Electronic computer conferencing (ECC) represents a further evolution of electronic message systems and provides a means of conducting asynchronous conversations with many participants. While an EMS can be used to conduct an electronic conversation involving many participants, the problems of carrying out many one-to-one conversations on a single topic produce a special variant of junk mail. Computer conferencing systems solve the junk mail problem by storing all messages on a given topic or from a given conference in such a way that all participants can see all messages. The system keeps track of each participant so that an individual who reenters the system is notified of any new messages since his or her last session. If a participant wishes to enter a new message, the system will inform other participants of this and other new messages. All old messages are kept for as long as the conference is active so that participants can easily review the conversations, search for specific messages, or reopen conversations that appear to have ended before suitable conclusions have been recorded.

Ideally, the micro is used as an intelligent terminal with the ability to store some material locally and to prepare text locally. Thus, the micro can be used to prepare one or several messages to be dispatched to the host when all messages are ready. Similarly, the local micro can be used to prepare drafts of reports or position papers that are to be developed jointly by several authors. The purpose of using the micro as an intelligent terminal is to minimize the costs of connecting to the main machine during text preparation. Once preparation or revision is complete, then the new draft is sent to the main machine so that the other authors can review it at their convenience. In this way, the micro, with computer conferencing facilities on a central computer, can be used to speed up the process of coming to a decision on a particular issue.

Research on the benefits and problems associated with computer conferencing facilities is now in progress. Computer conferencing has some substantial benefits over traditional meetings. Computer conferencing facilities reduce problems of distance, of setting a common meeting time, of obtaining floor time, and of wasting time listening to speeches. The major problems with electronic computer conferencing facilities relate to the availability of terminals and to widespread resistance to the use of keyboards.

Departmental Workstations and Electronic Forms

Departmental workstation is a collective term used to describe a micro installed to handle local record keeping, file storage, and information processing. Many other terms, including *intelligent terminal, information assistant,* and *smart desk,* have been used to describe the departmental workstation.

Electronic forms is another catchall term used to describe the mode of operation in the so-called paperless office. The multipart forms now used in most organizations can be replaced by electronic transactions with potentially many benefits: reduced errors, improved response time, and reduced effort for administrative activities. For example, a requisition for a new micro for the office of institutional research could be entered at a local departmental workstation to be stored in a record-keeping system. At the end of the day or at some other suitable time, all such electronic transactions would be sent to the appropriate office elsewhere in the institution. The requisition would go first to the purchasing office, which would review it and add whatever items were needed; then it would be sent on to accounts payable and out to the appropriate supplier in the form of a purchase order. (Most suppliers still need a paper form, but some are prepared to accept electronic orders.) Accounts payable would hold the transaction record until an invoice from the supplier was received and until the originating department sent electronic notification to indicate that the equipment had been installed.

The expectation is that electronic forms will be implemented through the use of appropriate software in both the departmental workstation and the central computer to provide for electronic transmission of information to handle requisitions, purchase orders, personnel appointments, and so on. The concept of electronic forms presumes that the systems being created also provide for appropriate feedback, that is, that they can acknowledge receipt of a form, ask for further information, provide notification of changes by the receiver, and so on.

The departmental workstation will have the capacity to cover the needs of particular departments in regard to local record-keeping problems. Many departments have unique problems in regard to common functions, such as financial information. With a departmental workstation, the department can summarize financial data in whatever way makes most sense to it. In this way, the department's needs are met, and the organization avoids having to build complex central systems that attempt to solve every conceivable problem. In contrast, central systems will be used to store the data needed by the organization as a whole. Some attention will be required to provide software that ensures synchronization of local data bases with corporate data bases.

One major problem remains to be overcome: Auditors and accountants are understandably nervous about electronic signatures. No widely acceptable solution is currently available, but many organizations have made much progress in regard to satisfactory electronic audit trails, control signatures, and passwords.

Local Area Networks

The benefits of the facilities just described require the micro to be connected to some sort of network. Various levels of networking can be implemented, ranging from truly local ones that connect a dozen offices on one floor of a building to organizational networks linking many buildings and to international public networks. Some local networks use one micro as a central control device. At the central micro, one usually finds a hard disk, a printer, and a plotter. The hard disk, a high-capacity nonremovable variant of the widely used floppy disk, is used to store the many files acquired by the various users of the network, and thus it is usually called a *file server*.

If the organization has an organizational network (another level of LAN), then the central micro just mentioned will include a gateway to the organizational network, and the organizational network may in turn include a gateway to one of the public networks. In this way, the users in a local network can have access to national bibliographical data bases, financial data bases, stock exchange data, and international electronic mail facilities.

The success of network projects depends to a large degree on the care with which the organization or institution follows current guidelines and standards. It is important to be aware that the International Standards Organization (ISO) has proposed a seven-layer control protocol for network communication. The lower layers specify the standards for the physical characteristics of the network, and the upper layers specify the communication protocols to be contained in software modules that must be implemented in the various computers that are to be connected. It is not essential to study and understand the ISO standards in depth, but it is important to know whether a network product being considered for purchase follows the standards, especially if it is likely that the network being planned will be connected to other local area networks in the institution or to public networks.

Networks are inevitably going to play an increasingly important role in institutional research. In individual institutions, networks are already being used to move data and information electronically from office to office in order to expedite the research and planning efforts of various constituencies. The same network may be used to conduct electronic conversations through electronic mail systems, computer conferencing facilities, or both. National networks can move data from one institution to another in support of the peer exchange activities that are becoming essential for planning activities. The national networks are also being used to handle electronic conversations, to conduct business meetings, and to expedite joint preparation of position papers to be used in discussions with government and other funding agencies.

Issues

Successful use of micros in communication activities depends on many facilities and individuals throughout the institution. A network facility is essential; ideally, it should be both robust and easy to use. Software facilities to handle electronic messages and computer conferencing are important. These facilities must be readily available on some reasonably central computer, which can be a minicomputer dedicated to a messaging service.

Planning for micros is particularly difficult because of the rapid developments now taking place. However, waiting for the industry to settle down is not a choice. There is much evidence that development will continue at a fast pace for many years. Institutions that plunge into the micro world typically do so with some specific arrangements. They choose two or three brands or models of micros and specify that all purchases must be from this selection. Alternatively, some institutions create the equivalent of an on-campus computer store, buying in quantity and offering units to departments or individuals at substantial discounts. The availability of in-house maintenance service serves to bring some measure of control. However, it is essential for the institution to review all control strategies thoroughly and frequently, because unforeseen new developments may become very important.

The problems of selecting microcomputer hardware may be somewhat eased if one recognizes that selection of a generic operating system is essential. Three operating systems are now in wide use: CP/M, produced by the Digital Research Corporation; UNIX, a product of Western Electric and Bell Labs; and MS-DOS, developed by Microsoft Corporation. CP/M became the standard operating system for eight-bit microcomputers; several versions are now available for sixteen-bit micros. UNIX was originally created for use on minicomputers, but it and many similar operating systems now exist for micros. MS-DOS was chosen by IBM as the operating system for the IBM Personal Computer, and it is now being used on many new microcomputers from other manufacturers. The choice of the operating system is important because the application software to be used in an office will be run under a given operating system. Thus, if one knows of some highly useful software that was designed to run under CP/M, it is essential to choose a micro that runs with CP/M.

Planning for networks is difficult; evolution is very rapid. In addition to separate data networks, organizations can now install integrated voice data (IVD) facilities so that voice and data communications can be handled through the same communication switch and telephone lines. All new telephone switches, also called private branch exchanges (PBXs) and computerized branch exchanges (CBXs), are computerized and offer a large range of new options. One of the more interesting options is voice mail, a form of electronic mail in which voice messages are stored and replayed to recipients when they telephone in to check their mail. As this option becomes more widely available, it will compete with the electronic mail systems described earlier.

In some organizations, technical planning is now being done in a six-month time frame in recognition of the perception that the half-life of new developments in high-tech areas is about six months. Coordination of all planning for communications is important if an organization is to take advantage of the departmental workstation. The data network is usually the responsibility of the computing center, while the telephone network and campus mail may be the responsibility of administrative services, and the personnel department may be in charge of staff training. All these groups must be in agreement if the new technologies are to be successfully integrated into the organization's communication channels, both formal and informal.

Some departments and individuals will join new technologies with very high expectations. Training will be required to initiate individuals and offices. However, some training effort should also be directed toward containing the unbounded enthusiasm of recent converts. While some enthusiasm is essential, the fanatics will be perceived as such, and this could cause backlash problems elsewhere in the institution. Thus, implementation of micros, networks, and electronic mail systems requires much careful attention to ensure that the expectations for these new technologies are realistic.

A staged approach to the implementation of micros is believed to be essential in order to capitalize on new developments and to avoid long-term commitment to an approach that may become impractical. Some experimentation may be advisable. Different departments within an institution may be permitted, even encouraged, to try different hardware and software environments in order for the institution to gain wide experience.

Despite the cautionary nature of the points just made, it is important to stress that the rapid spread and increasing use of micros are inevitable. The purpose of these caveats is to reinforce the need for careful planning and coordination if the maximum benefit is to be obtained from this versatile and powerful new tool. In Chapter Six of this volume, Vinod Chachra amplifies on these issues.

Derek M. Jamieson is research adviser to the president at the University of Guelph. He is currently on the staff of the Bovey Commission, which is studying proposals to rationalize the university system in Ontario.

Kenneth H. MacKay is data resource administrator at the University of Guelph, where he is responsible for the coordination of all its computerized administrative systems.

For equivalent computer power, smaller computers are not more expensive than larger computers. The cost of computing in the immediate future will be governed not by hardware costs but rather by personnel, software, and communications costs.

Micros, Minis, and Mainframes

Vinod Chachra

The decade of the eighties represents a new era in computing. The widespread availability and use of microcomputers—popularly known in industry as *personal computers*—has permanently altered our view of computing. Month by month, the scene in the computer industry changes. Announcements of new products and enhancements of existing products offer opportunities and options that alter the parameters of the campus computing equation. Change constantly threatens the best plans, forever urging renewed consideration of the available options. In the late sixties and up until the middle seventies, the use of computing was governed by the economics of size. During that period, Herbert Grosch presented an idea that became known as Grosch's Law (Solomon, 1966). He claimed that the power of computing varies as the square of the price. Grosch's Law was a good predictor of price performance at that time. Some claim that computer manufacturers thought the law was very reasonable and set their prices accordingly. The fact remains that for twice the price one could buy four times the computing power. Those days are gone.

The introduction of mini- and microcomputers, coupled with recent dramatic price decreases, has all but negated Grosch's Law. Currently, for equivalent computer power, smaller computers are no more expensive than larger computers. Is it better to buy a large number of smaller computers or a small number of larger computers? How many mainframes, minis, and micros should an organization own? When are five minis better than one mainframe? When are fifty micros better than one mini?

The answers to these questions are not as straightforward as they once were. Arguments in favor of one or a few large computers point to increased efficiency of machine and personnel, larger capacity, and shared software. Among the disadvantages of larger systems are greater overhead costs, larger incremental expansion, and greater impact of equipment failures. Whereas centralization and decentralization seem to represent only two choices, there are in fact three choices: centralization, decentralization, and centralization with decentralized access. Other combinations can certainly be defined, but for most large campuses, there is a need for the entire range of computing resources. The most important factors in answering this question are personnel and software costs, for the cost of computing in the immediate future will be governed not by hardware costs but rather by personnel, software, and communication costs.

The primary objective of the analysis that follows is to provide readers with a better understanding of the factors that influence the selection of one type of computer over another. While there is no single solution common to every case, there are some general principles that can be applied to most situations. These general principles are the subject of this discussion, where I have attempted to present a framework for the review, analysis, and understanding of computing options.

The best characterization of computing that I have seen so far follows from McKeefery's (1973) proposal that one way of measuring the value and impact of a new technology is to see by what factor it has multiplied human capabilities to do a given task. For example, modern jet transportation, which reaches a speed of 600 miles per hour, is 150 times the speed of walking, so it is a 150-factor multiplier. Automobiles moving at sixty miles an hour are a 15-factor multiplier over walking. The invention of the plow for tilling was only a tenfold improvement over previously known methods. The wheel represented a tenfold improvement over previously known techniques of moving materials. Occasionally in history, certain technologies present much higher factors of multiplication. For instance, the steam engine, which ushered in the great Industrial Revolution, was a thousandfold multiplier. There have even been some million multipliers. The first such million multiplier was in communication technology. By means first of wires, then of wireless, then of television, we learned to send messages across the world a million times faster than we ever had before. Atomic energy and its destructive power was the second million multiplier that we have known. The third million multiplier is obviously the computer.

What is truly significant is that, for the first time in human history, we are able to multiply the million multiplier a million times by bringing communications and computers together. It is not possible even to project what the impact on our lives will be from this millionfold multiplication of a million multiplier. The advancements we are seeing today do not begin to represent the possibilities that are sure to exist in the future. Interestingly enough, what started out to be a nuclear age is now an information age.

Industry Perspectives

Hardware. In 1980, approximately half the cost of running a computing service could be attributed to hardware costs and the other half to software and personnel costs. Since then, the cost of hardware has dropped by 20 percent a year, and the cost of software and personnel has risen at the rate of about 10 percent a year. Various studies indicate that this trend will continue or even accelerate. Under these assumptions, we may conclude that by 1990 approximately 10 percent of the total cost of computing will be attributed to hardware and approximately 90 percent to software and personnel. Of course, such projections may never materialize, because changing economics could alter consumer behavior to the point that the problem itself is no longer the same. Given this caveat, what courses of action do these cost projections call for?

The useful life of equipment should not be taken to be longer than five years, with four years the more reasonable figure, and three years the most likely. Although computers are theoretically built to last forever, such factors as technological obsolescence, increased maintenance, and operational costs preclude a longer useful life. For instance, an IBM 370-158 requires five times as much power as the IBM 4341, and it generates five times the amount of heat. At today's prices, the total difference in cost of electricity can be around $12,000 a year. The differences in air conditioning and maintenance costs are substantially larger. The analysis is similar for smaller systems, although it would take a collection of one or two thousand personal computers to produce a financial impact of the same order of magnitude.

Only a part of the improvement in price performance of any computer will come from improved technology; the rest will come from economies of scale, not of size. Thus, unless overriding considerations stipulate otherwise, the products that have — or that have the potential of having — a large installed-base should be chosen.

The drop in hardware prices is not limited to the central processing unit. Disk systems are experiencing similar price drops. As disk storage systems become cheaper, the function of tape systems for the storage of user data will be greatly reduced. Tape systems will be used primarily for backup and archival purposes. The operating system resides in virtual memory; the user program resides in virtual memory; perhaps the time has come for user data to reside in virtual memory. Whereas tape systems are still in use for large systems and to some extent for minicomputers, they have become almost extinct for personal computers.

Software. Software costs are continuing to rise. One manufacturer increased the price of its operating system by a factor of ten in one year. Advances in software development techniques have fallen far behind advances in hardware technology. Software development continues to be a very labor-intensive process, and programmer productivity, in spite of all the tools now available in the marketplace, has not improved substantially. Industry estimates indicate that programmer productivity has improved an average of 3 percent a year. Software maintenance also continues to be a very time-consuming and expensive process. Thus, software costs are very closely linked to personnel costs. One notable exception is application software for microcomputers. This is true because the market for microcomputers is very large and because a substantial portion of microcomputer software is developed by hobbyists in their spare time. Microcomputer software is still a cottage industry, and thus it is still relatively inexpensive.

Personnel. The acute shortage of personnel in computer-related areas is projected to continue for several years, at least through the mid eighties. The shortage is already escalating salaries, which are expected to increase much faster than the inflation rate. Several institutions are reexamining their compensation programs for computer-related titles with a view to bringing them more in line with those in the business world. Failure to do so will simply cause institutions to become training grounds for organizations able to offer more attractive compensation packages.

The salary issue has yet another dimension. The salary commanded by a systems analyst may easily exceed that of a tenured assistant professor or a director of personnel. Data processing directors command even higher salaries, sometimes as high as that of the president of a small institution. These higher salaries can cause serious discontent among other professionals in the institution. Structured salary scales cannot always accommodate these differences. These concerns are part of the reason why some institutions have contracted for the management of their computer facilities. The contractor receives a consulting fee and hires the individuals necessary to provide the services. The institution therefore does not have to carry these disproportionately higher-paid individuals on its payroll.

In summary, then, the cost of hardware will continue to decline while the cost of personnel and software will continue to rise. Hence, the proper management strategy in using various sizes of computers must be based on the impact that they will have on overall personnel and software requirements and the resultant costs. The recommendations in this chapter on the use of different types of computers are based on this perspective.

Mainframes, Minis, and Micros

As the use of mini and micro systems continues to grow, it becomes necessary to identify the application areas where one system is clearly superior to the others.

Mainframes. As a general rule, large shared computers should be used for the following purposes: for number crunching in large-scale computational problems; under certain data requirements—for large amounts of data, for small amounts of data shared with large groups, and for data archiving; with specialized software; and with special devices, such as laser printers and flatbed printers.

The application of mainframes to large computational needs is self-evident. When problems become so large that they take inordinate amounts of time on smaller machines, then mainframes become the clear choice.

The application of mainframes for data handling situations is less evident. Clearly, when large amounts of data, such as census data or library data, need to be processed, the mainframe is again the best choice. Applications for mainframes when small amounts of data are involved are less apparent. When one group needs to know instantaneously any changes made by another group—for example, "drop/adds," student accounting, airline reservations—large shared computers are the obvious choice although the amount of data to be shared may not be significant. Data archiving by definition implies large shared systems.

Some software can be run only on larger machines. Examples are simulation packages, mathematical packages (MPSX and others), data base packages (ADABAS, IMS), and special compilers (SNOBOL, LISP). For these specialized packages, the choice is clear. In other cases where the software can be run on a smaller machine, it may be too expensive to duplicate it on multiple machines, hence it may be desirable to share it on a single larger machine. For example, if the FORTRAN compiler costs $300 and there are 2,000 micros that need it, the total cost can be $600,000.

Such special devices as laser printers, flatbed plotters, and computer output microfiche (COM) are examples of expensive special devices that are economically operated only on large shared systems where the volume of usage can justify the corresponding expense. These are the only significant reasons for using large systems. All other applications can be done better on other types of machines that more closely meet the specific needs of individual users.

Minicomputers. Minicomputers, particularly the superminis, are now approaching mainframe capacities. Minis today sport large memory capacity and high-speed processors, and they have the ability to accommodate complex needs. The total hardware costs for minis are generally lower than the costs for mainframes, but personnel costs can remain high because operators, maintenance work, and user services are all required. In order to reduce personnel costs, the use of minicomputers should be governed by their impact on personnel costs. As a general rule, minicomputers should be used in three situations: in sponsored research projects where the sponsor so designates; in environments where the software requirement is very limited (for example, seismic data analysis), where the clientele is very restricted (for example, CAD/CAM image processing), and where the machine can run essentially unattended; where minicomputers can be acquired and supported through departmental budgets, research contracts, or gifts. In the last case, departments should provide a personnel impact statement prior to acquisition of the minicomputer so that the total system costs can be assessed accurately.

Whereas there is no clear-cut general recommendation, it can be shown that minicomputers are extremely cost-effective if they can be dedicated to single application areas running a single software package. Examples in research computing include very large-scale integrated (VLSI) circuit design and seismic data analysis. Examples in administrative processing include library automation, food service management, and medical record keeping. Note particularly that none of these applications requires any degree of data sharing with other institutional applications, such as payroll, student records, and so forth.

Microcomputers. Microcomputers, like minis and mainframes, can be used for instruction, research, and administrative purposes. However, the number acquired for research and administrative purposes is certain to be smaller than the number acquired for instructional purposes.

The reasons usually cited for the acquisition of microcomputers are ease of use, low cost, full control, independence from external priority or influence, portability, and other user convenience. However, the most urgent reason for the acquisition of microcomputers comes from the potential they offer in changing the device-to-port ratio, that is, the number of devices that can be served by access ports to a mainframe computer. Virginia Tech, for example, has approximately 2,100 devices (terminals, micros, and so forth) and 1,000 access ports. Networking techniques and port allocation machines (port contending switches) permit the number of computer ports to be somewhat lower than the number of devices. As a general rule, each port can easily support two to three terminals. Thus, the device-to-port ratio varies between two to one and three to one for acceptable levels of service.

It is projected that the number of devices on campus at Virginia Tech will near 4,000 next year and reach 6,000 by 1986. Under present device-to-port ratios, this projected increase would require in excess of 2,000 computer ports. Two thousand computer ports and the necessary communication and computer capacity to support them will be prohibitively expensive. Hence, as the number of devices increases, the device-to-port ratio needs to be increased significantly. The desired results can be achieved by using microcomputers networked to the mainframe. Professionals hope that, through the use of microcomputers, the ratio of devices to ports can approach ten to one, thus yielding a fivefold increase. Will the microcomputers reduce the load on the mainframe? It is anticipated that the overall work load on the mainframe will increase rather than decrease, although the type of work will change substantially.

The technical and managerial issues associated with microcomputers are very important. However, perhaps the most important issue in large organizations involves the acquisition and management of software. Assume that the campus population of faculty, staff, and students collectively purchases 2,000 microcomputers. Assume further that each system requires an expensive applications package that costs somewhere between $300 and $500. Simple multiplication reveals that between $600,000 and $1,000,000 can be invested in software alone unless alternate strategies are sought and implemented.

At that price, the development of software for in-house consumption becomes an attractive prospect. Clearly the marketplace cannot tolerate a situation in which large institutions like Virginia Tech are compelled to develop their own software. Hence, one must conclude that suppliers of software will make attractive volume or educational discounts. It should be institutional policy to seek out attractive financial arrangements for the acquisition of software. This is the most important activity in the implementation of microcomputers—even more important than the negotiation of attractive hardware prices.

Types of Computing

Any university community is generally served by four types of computing service: personal, local, departmental, and global. Each has its own particular characteristics that suggest the optimum type of computer configuration.

Personal Computing. Personal computing consists of devices owned and operated by individuals. These devices—typically computers or terminals—can be located in offices or in homes. It is frequently a university's policy to permit the connection of these devices to the university-owned computer for the conduct of university-related activities from the homes of faculty, staff, and students. Although this is not a radical accommodation due to existing dial-up access, a problem can be created when the university begins to build a local area network (LAN) that forces consideration of access from student dormitories and faculty homes. In addition to the increase in the sheer number of users, a LAN arrangement requires special wiring and control devices in lieu of telephone lines and dial-up access ports.

Local Computing. Local computing involves devices that are purchased by individuals or by a department and located in a laboratory or assigned to a faculty member. Data acquisition systems, process control devices, personal computers, word processing stations, and terminals make up the major applications in this group. Local computers are restricted-access facilities—usually dedicated to the use of a single individual—and costs are usually borne by the department.

Departmental Computing. Departmental computing consists of the systems owned and operated by departments and used by a small and clearly identified group, such as a team working on a given research project, members of a specific class, or persons associated with a specific department. Generally, departmental computing is dedicated to a single function and uses limited-access facilities consisting of minis, micros, terminals, and so forth. Typically, departmental computing is supported with departmental operating funds.

Global Computing. Global computing consists of the systems that are owned and operated by the university as a service to the entire university community. Typically, these general-purpose, multifunction, open-access facilities consist of large computers, minicomputers, micros, terminals, and other specialized devices, such as printers, readers, and plotters. Global computing utilizes unrestricted-access facilities that are shared by all users in the community.

Charging for Computing

Another interesting consideration is the impact that the deployment of micros, minis, or mainframes may have on charging and cost recovery algorithms. The appropriate charging scheme depends on the mode of computing operation. In a generalized sense, one can view computing as existing in three modes: library, job shop, and utility. The initial mode of computer use was probably similar to library service: Users checked out the computer for their exclusive use, much as they checked out a library book. The emergence of the microcomputer has resulted in a resurgence of demand for such hands-on use of computers. The library usage was followed by job shop and utility modes, and with the microcomputer we come full circle in usage patterns.

The job shop takes the pattern of the manufacturing industry. This industry has rather conclusively demonstrated that, where the machine is the critical resource, job shop scheduling techniques can produce significant economies in production. A job shop is characterized by an operation where the user brings the data, and the computing center does whatever is necessary to produce the results. The user is concerned only with the results, not with the details of processing. The management of a job shop requires scheduled run times, prespecified resource requirements, and predetermined priorities. Service charging in the job shop mode is probably best handled by unit charges assessed on the user's view of the output, that is, checks written, invoices printed, ledger items posted, and so forth. In such an environment, the center can and should be held responsible for the accurate and timely processing of data, but it should not be held responsible for the accuracy of the results. Late submissions cannot be expected to gain time at the center. The dismal history of the data processing job shop leaves one wondering whether this mode of operation will ever work smoothly in any but the smallest computer centers.

In contrast, the utility mode treats the computer center much like the power company. The appliance that the user plugs into a power outlet is of no concern to the power company so long as voltage and current specifications are not violated. In a computing environment operated as a utility, the center provides only the computer power, the storage, and the output. What programs are run and what data are used become the exclusive responsibility of the user. In the utility mode, the center charges for the actual resources used. It has no concern either with the programs that are run or with the results that are produced. The responsibility is to provide good raw computer power, no more and no less.

The library mode of operation does not lend itself to charging at all, particularly if the computer in use is a microcomputer. This mode is recommended by those who argue that in an institution of higher education the computer and the library are both important information resources and should be operated similarly, that is, at no cost to users. However, there are significant differences. First, in a library, the proportion of resources in use at any one time (books in use or checked out) is small compared to the total available resources. For free computing to be possible, the available capacity would have to be significantly greater than the capacity required by peak load demands. Such excess is not likely to be encountered in the near future; most campuses will have to make major increases in their computational capacity just to accommodate peak load demands. Second, the library has no consumable resources directly associated with its service, since a book is read, returned, and reread. In contrast, computers use up paper, ribbons, cards, ink, plotter pens, and so forth as a direct result of resource availability. Even if the computer processing were free, the consumables would have to be charged to users. Third, computer time is a resource that resembles an airline seat: If it is not filled at the appropriate time, it cannot be used at all. Fourth, libraries are generally considered to be open-access facilities for public good, on the conviction that a free and democratic society requires an informed and educated population. In contrast, computers are controlled-access facilities, because the demand for services appears to be insatiable. It is this attribute that allows universities to charge sponsored research projects directly for computer use but not for library use.

It seems a worthy aspiration to make computers absolutely free to all users. However, as long as computing resources are scarce, they will continue to be subject to some form of resource management and control requirements. The choice of an appropriate form of resource management is critical to the success of the computing enterprise.

Managing Decentralization

There are three principal players in the game of computing on campus: the computing center, the departments, and individual computer owners. Each party owns some computational capacity. In order to facilitate the proper use of mainframes, minis, and micros, each player must understand and respect the role of the other players. The key to such understanding and to effective coordination is the particular model used for management of computing on campus. This section presents guidelines for developing a successful model.

The Computing Center. It should be the responsibility of the computing center to acquire, maintain, and operate all global facilities for computing. The global facility will consist of several shared computers. No other organization within the campus may own or operate global facilities. All global facilities are centrally managed. Thus, a separate center for research or administrative computing is not recommended. In addition, the computing center should have responsibility for operating a campuswide data network supporting all computers of any type or size.

The computing center should operate the global facilities under a set of performance standards and operating policies defined by the computer policy committee. The computing center should report on a regular basis, but no less than quarterly, the performance it has achieved relative to the standards specified by the computer policy committee. From time to time, the computing center should bring to the attention of the computer policy committee such recommendations (including major equipment acquisitions or upgrades) as may be necessary to continue to meet the standards specified by the policy committee.

The computing center may, at the request of the department and on approval by the policy committee, agree to perform the facilities management function for departmental computing on a full cost recovery basis. The computing center should have no responsibility for development of applications software. It should be responsible only for maintenance of general-purpose application packages. The computing center should maintain usage statistics on these packages and report them regularly to the user community. The computing center should interact regularly with user groups and keep written minutes of its deliberations. The computing center should assume no responsibility for user programs or user data. It should operate as a utility except for its microcomputer service, which should operate like a library.

The computing center should earmark a certain portion of its budget for nonrecoverable services in support of general-purpose microcomputer laboratories, classrooms equipped with terminals, or a general-purpose broadband data network capable of connecting several thousand devices. The computing center budget should be determined at the beginning of each year and remain fixed for the balance of the year. The facilities operated and managed by the computing center do not necessarily have to be located at a single site. Clearly, by definition, the computing center operates a combined (but not necessarily centralized) facility for the university serving general-purpose research, academic, and administrative needs. Thus, the role of the computing center is not necessarily to own equipment but rather to provide management, training, and access services to the community.

The Department. It should be the responsibility of the department to acquire, maintain, and run local and departmental facilities. As a general rule, the departmental facility should consist of a single-purpose minicomputer running a single software system, (such as image processing, CAD/CAM, seismic analysis, and so forth). Because the cost of computing is dominated by personnel and software costs, departmental computers need not show a utilization of 100 percent capacity. Instead, the objective should be to minimize software and operational costs.

It should be the policy of the university not to charge for the use of local computing facilities, but it should be the policy of the university to develop a charging algorithm for departmental facilities. However, these charges should be levied only against noninstitutional users and externally sponsored programs. As a general rule, departmental facilities should not sell computer time to others outside the department except in the case of joint research projects. (The rationale here is to prevent the proliferation of computing facilities, each having expensive support staff.)

Departments may, on a full cost recovery basis, contract with the computing center to operate and manage their departmental facility. Departments unable to sustain their departmental facilities through departmental funds may choose to assign the equipment as a global facility with access privileges to all. The facility would then be managed and operated by the computing center.

Individual Users. Individual owners of personal computers will have an increasing influence on campus computing. Improbable as it may seem, it is neither desirable nor necessary to mandate that all individual users purchase the same personal computer. Such a requirement can only place unnecessary constraints on the creative instincts of faculty and students. However, as a practical matter, it is not possible for the computing center to provide consulting help, support services, hardware and software evaluation, and other networking services for a large number of incompatible systems. Whereas it is not necessary for an institution to require all faculty and staff to use the same machines, it is necessary for the institution to select one, two, or three different personal computer systems that it is able to support. Experimentation with nonsupported systems should be encouraged with the clear understanding that the users are on their own. In research situations or with sophisticated users, this is not a matter of concern.

Software will be a critical resource in the effective use of personal computers. Efforts should be made to permit an exchange among users of their acquired experience with software packages, applications programs, or both. A user group or a centralized library of software should be maintained.

The purpose of personal computing is to permit users to create an environment of computing that suits their individual personalities and that is customized for the intended use. Thus, users should have the liberty to choose any software that best meets their needs. However, computing is more than an individual activity. It is also a social phenomenon. Experience indicates that personal computer users very soon begin to interact with other personal computer users, exchanging products or working together on the same activity. This interactive form of usage requires certain common and supported protocols in order to accomplish the necessary communication. It is here that individual interests must be compromised in favor of the common purpose. The computing center should specify standards and, if possible, provide interfaces to permit the users of personal computers to access a network. It should be possible for the personal computer user to access the campus network without undue syntactic, communications, linguistic, accounting, and procedural constraints from a centralized network controller.

This concept of operations may be summarized as follows: First, users may choose any personal computer that best meets their needs and any software that best defines the environment in which they wish to operate. Second, the computing center should support a limited number of different microcomputers. For the computers supported, the center should negotiate master software contracts, provide network interfaces, coordinate maintenance, and provide consulting and education services. Third, users should register any new and unique software system with the library or with the computing center library. Users should have the ability to check out a software package from the library for testing and evaluation purposes. Such copies of software can be abbreviated versions of the total package. Fourth, the center should strive to create an environment in which the users of personal computers can process their work on their own machine or transfer the work to some other machine connected to the network for completion. This requires support at four levels: stand-alone operation, terminal emulation operations, file transfer operations, and network service operations. Each level requires greater sophistication than the preceding level. Fifth, personal computers should be available for dedicated personal use. However, it is desirable to have a shared facility consisting of several personal computers equipped with special devices or software that individuals are unable or unwilling to duplicate. Such a central facility would qualify as a global facility, and it should operate under the guidelines previously specified.

Conclusion

Is it better to buy a large number of small computers or a small number of large computers? The answer is not easy or straightforward. This chapter has outlined the applications for which each type of computer — mainframe, minicomputer, and microcomputer — is more appropriate. How many of each type one should acquire depends largely on the objectives to be achieved. Grosch's Law is no longer valid. Hence, there is no economic incentive to buy larger computers rather than smaller ones. Because of reduced personnel costs, microcomputers can in fact be more cost-effective, provided that the job is small enough to be executed on a microcomputer and that the necessary software is already available on the system. Computer planning is no longer driven by the costs of hardware but rather by personnel and software considerations. Planning decisions should therefore be based primarily on their impact on personnel and software costs.

How much computing is enough? Demand for computing seems insatiable. Thus, it is safe to say that, when available capacity exceeds peak load demand, we have sufficient computer capacity. Peak demand in an organization is determined by users' view of the computer. The computer can be considered a number cruncher, a word processor, a symbol manipulator, a media converter, or an extension of the thought process. The amount of computing needed depends on the perspective. For the average user, a saturation level is reached when about 30 percent of working time is spent directly with the machine.

The type of computing one needs—mainframe, mini, or micro—depends on the application. Just as passenger cars, vans, and trucks coexist on the highway system, so also must mainframes, minis, and micros coexist within the intellectual domain, each to serve a useful function.

References

McKeefery, W. J. "The Million Multipliers." *Proceedings of the 1973 CAUSE National Conference*. Boulder, Colo.: CAUSE, 1973.

Solomon, M. B. "The Economics of Scale and the IBM System 360." *Communications of the ACM*. New York: Association for Computing Machinery (ACM), Inc., 1966.

Vinod Chachra is vice-president for computing and information systems at Virginia Polytechnic Institute and State University. As a consultant, he has shared his expertise in management of computing and in library automation with institutions in the United States, Australia, and South America. Recently, he received the CAUSE Award for Exemplary Leadership in the field of higher education information systems.

Decision support systems hold great promise, but the key to their success will be effective decision support management. Institutional researchers are well suited to undertake this function.

The Case for Decision Support Management

Paul Jedamus

In northeastern Colorado a few years ago, an old hard-scrabbling bachelor was eking out a living on his small, soil- and water-poor spread, living, in a manner of speaking, on beans and jackrabbits. Then, oil was discovered on his property, and he became an instant millionaire. Two years later, not believing what had happened, he was still living on beans and jackrabbits. The distributed computing, telematic revolution is not coming, it is here. But, most administrators in higher education are still living on beans and jackrabbits. And that is too bad, because the possibilities of the new world that is upon us are not being exploited to our advantage.

Further, the changes that are implicit in this new age are not just incremental improvements on past processes. Many administrators seem to believe that the sum and substance of the new computer-based technology is the use of spreadsheet modeling languages to answer quickly such what-if questions as, What would our net income be if freshman enrollment dropped 10 percent from last year while salary costs increased 5 percent? and to conduct such goal seeks as determining the level at which tuition has to be set in order to break even, given the changes just described. However, just as the development of the automobile not only provided a way to get from here to there faster but also changed the economic and social structure of the nation, so it is with the development of computers. On line what-ifs and goal seeks make life easier now, but they are also part of a revolution that has far greater implications.

This revolution may well change the organizational structure of higher education as well as the way in which problems are perceived and decisions are made. Such changes will come about because networks of micros, each with the computing power of past mainframes, and new modeling languages are enabling us for the first time to make use of the power of decision support systems (DSSs).

Significant DSS capabilities are already here. Individual administrators at a single location or decision center can use them effectively with no more than a few days of experimentation. These isolated applications of decision support, called specific decision support systems (SDSSs), do not require in-house development of expensive software. Their capabilities and ease of application can be illustrated by our experience at the University of Colorado–Boulder. There, neophyte M.B.A. students learn to combine their judgment with powerful analytic tools to make business decisions. For example, using the Blear Company, an integrative illustration (Plane, forthcoming), students and their professor together develop an SDSS that not only uses what-ifs and goal seeks to advantage but also incorporates linear and nonlinear optimization, multiple nonlinear regression analysis, and Monte Carlo simulation. Supported by appropriate software accessed through an interactive computer terminal and displayed with a large-screen projector, the appropriate models are developed and manipulated during a single class session.

The full potential of decision support is realized when SDSSs are interwoven into a comprehensive network. Construction of such a network is necessary to reap the huge potential benefits of DSSs, but the process is difficult. Problems that can be encountered, how these problems must be overcome through decision support management, and the part that institutional research can play in the process are the central themes of this chapter. However, before addressing these themes, we must explore in some depth the structure of DSSs in higher education.

The Structure of Decision Support Systems in Higher Education

Decision support systems "provide an integrative computer-based system designed to assist decision makers (including groups) in using data and models to address semistructured or unstructured problems or decisions that have implications for the effectiveness of the organization. Decision support systems are intended to provide the administrator or manager with direct, flexible, easy-to-use computer-based support for important nonroutine problems and decisions and are designed to enhance judgment rather then replace it" (Norris and Mims, 1984, p. 11).

In the view of many experts, the chief use to which microcomputer networks will be put is the development and use of DSSs for strategic and tactical planning and sometimes even for operational control. According to Keen and

Scott-Morton (1978), "decision support systems represent a point of view on the role of the computer in the management decision-making process. Decision support implies the use of computers to: (1) assist managers in their decision processes in semistructured tasks; (2) support, rather than replace, managerial judgment; (3) improve the effectiveness of decision making rather than its efficiency."

Sprague and Carlson (1982) stress the use of iterative design in the development of adaptive decision support systems. In this process, they identify five key roles: the users of specific decision support systems; intermediaries to assist them if necessary; the builders of the decision support generator, that is, of the specific hardware and software configuration necessary to provide users with easy access to relevant data and appropriate methods of analysis; the technical supporter, who develops new hardware and software capabilities; and the toolsmith, who builds linkages betwen subsystems. Both Sprague and Carlson (1982) and others describe in detail how these tasks are performed, who in the organization performs them, and how they are coordinated. Thierauf (1982) provides case studies to document how various companies have built DSS generators, some of which proved to be applicable beyond the company itself; developed feasibility studies for DSS by organizing an executive steering committee, a user review group, and a project team; and measured costs and benefits for each potential DSS alternative.

However, that is not how decision support systems will be built at most institutions of higher education. First, there will be no in-house builders of the decision support generator. It is far too expensive and time-consuming, and most institutions lack the necessary personnel. Powerful commercial DSS generators are now available at far less cost then it takes to build one from scratch. They will quickly become even more powerful and less expensive. The information gained in their use will be transferable among institutions that use the same generator. This will promote the sharing of knowledge about how best to install and use the generators, and it will permit persons skilled in their use to move from one institution to another.

Second, companies that produce DSS generators are also proficient in teaching potential customers how to use them. Some such companies also offer special incentives to colleges and universities to expose students to their use. Execucom Systems Corporation (1983), for example, now has 152 colleges and universities in North America and 53 in other countries using interactive financial planning simulations (IFPSs) in business courses under its subsidized university support program. The result is likely to be the creation of a cadre of trained graduates who are enthusiastic and knowledgeable about the use of IFPSs. Some of these graduates will become executives and managers. Advantages accrue not only to the company that sells the service but also to the organizations that employ the students.

Third, most colleges and universities have neither the time nor the funds to mount a full-fledged, organizationwide effort to develop a comprehensive decision support system. Rather, such development will be incremental. Using a commercial generator, a few individuals or a small group will develop a small, operational specific decision support system. Once the advantages become obvious, as they will, the SDSSs will proliferate, and eventually they will grow into a full DSS. But, it is crucial for the growth not to be haphazard; effective management of the process is imperative.

Fourth, the literature on DSS emphasizes that its main use lies in strategic planning, where the decision-making process is relatively unstructured, and that it relies to a great extent on exogenous sources of information, although some applications are made in the areas of tactical planning and operational control.

Strategic planning involves the setting of policies, the choice of objectives, the selection of resources, long-range forecasting, and the evaluation of plans of action. Tactical planning (or management control) includes short-range forecasting as well as the making of decisions to assure effectiveness in the acquisition and use of resources. Operational control involves making decisions to assure effectiveness in the conduct of operations (Sprague and Carlson, 1982).

In illustrating the differences among these three types of functions, current tests rely on the classical organizational pyramid for business operations. This model works well for the traditional manufacturing company, but it is unrealistic for companies relying on high levels of research and technology. Although it is appropriate enough for the business functions of an institution of higher education, it is very inappropriate for its academic aspects. A much more realistic model for academic decision making is shown in Figure 1. In this model, the traditional notions of top-down, grass roots, and management levels are inappropriate. All three types of planning and control are performed by faculty members, department heads, deans, chancellor, and governing board—though in different proportions—at each of the various decision centers.

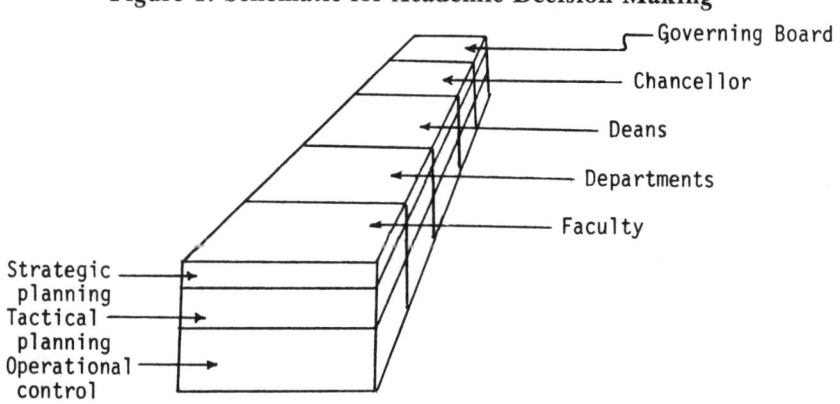

Figure 1. Schematic for Academic Decision Making

To illustrate, surely a Nobel prizewinner in, say, molecular and cellular biology spends a good deal of time in strategic planning—probably more than a harried chancellor busy with the day's imperatives. He chooses research objectives as his field of study and his own creativity leads him, he evaluates alternative plans of action, he secures material and human resources through grants and appropriations, and he engages in long-range forecasting.

In reviewing the annual report of M.I.T. president Paul E. Gray, *Technology Review* ("Can We Turn Down the Heat on the Faculty?" 1984, p. 78) notes that, "as it turns out, faculty members are responsible for obtaining grants to support most of the research that brings distinction to M.I.T. Some of that grant money typically covers a portion of professors' own salaries as well as stipends for graduate and postdoctoral—and sometimes undergraduate—students. Last year, says Gray, the average faculty member in a field where sponsored research is a major factor raised $300,000. The process—the result of a vast amount of discussion and proposal writing—involves 'an extraordinary amount of time and energy.'"

In contrast, the typical dean spends much time in tactical planning and management control. Historically, it is probably fair to say that boards of governors and legislative committees spend a disproportionate amount of time on short-range forecasting related to financial matters, on articulating their personal educational philosophies or political objectives, and even on dictating methods of operational control.

Even in the highly structured business organizational model, authorities agree that the notion of distributed data bases is an integral part of distributed computing. Each decision center that is the site of an SDSS needs a particular set of information inputs, both indigenous and exogenous, to generate appropriate decision alternatives. But, in an integrated decision support system, decisions made at one decision center become data at other centers. This is particularly important in the academic environment where strategic planning is dispersed. Thus, managing the coordination of specific decision support systems into an overall system is crucial.

Toward Information Anarchy?

Times have surely changed. Getting enough information on which to base dcisions was once a difficult task. The problem now lies in identifying, amid the plethora of information sources, those that are most meaningful to the application at hand. We have moved from the problem of how to make decisions with limited information to the equally vexing problem of how to make decisions with practically unlimited information.

For exogenous information, there are literally thousands of on line data bases accessible for a fee. They cover everything from market shares for dogfood to medical diagnoses. There are dozens of data bases on higher education, and both their scope and their accessibility increase daily. How good are they? Previously, when an analyst known and trusted by the decision maker obtained entire budgets from a selected group of institutions and carefully spent days making comparative budget analyses, the decision maker could be sure that the data were comparable. Now, in spite of widespread systematic efforts to ensure comparability, relying on data generated by others is essentially an act of faith.

For a reasonable fee, many data base specialty firms will perform analyses as well. How good are they? Some will project an institution's enrollments using only recent past enrollment. At least that option eliminates the problem of assessing the effects of incipient exogenous change. One firm of high repute produced statewide long-term enrollment forecasts using a multiple regression model in which one of the independent variables was a projection of unemployment in that state five years into the future. When asked how that particular variable was itself predicted, the response was that, since everyone knew there would be variation about the trend of the number of unemployed, an arbitrary cycle had been imposed.

Problems of this nature are accentuated because inaccuracies in data and circumspect analyses can have a multiplicative effect. When any decision center has access to myriad data sources, the data used at one center can become embedded in data bases constructed at other centers. As the data-decisions cycle is repeated, long forgotten or never realized inaccuracies become part of another decision maker's facts. Measuring standard errors under these circumstances is impossible.

There are also problems with internally generated data. With distributed data bases, who if anyone controls data input? Does a chief information officer (CIO) coordinate data definitions and entry? In a sense, data are artifacts of our perceptions and perhaps of our aspirations. Much like the different descriptions of the same accident given by different witnesses, where each person truly believes that what he or she saw was what actually happened, data can become official simply because a particular definition reinforces some decision maker's perspective. This could lead to resentment and lack of cooperation from affected parties who feel that their definitions are not only as valid but better. It could also generate black market data that effectively circumvent policy dictates.

All these factors could lead to what I have described as information anarchy (Hample, 1983). Inconsistent internal information and divergent external data bases may with the best of intentions be used to generate models that are inaccurate or inappropriate. Separate decision centers provided with awesome computing capabilities and communication networks but saturated with an overabundance of unarticulated bits and pieces can paste together a hodgepodge of SDSSs. Even though individual decision centers access accurate and timely information, lack of effective communication among centers may well lead to overall suboptimization. The only solution is effective decision support management.

Decision Support Management and Institutional Research

Decision support management (DSM) is the process by which specific decision support systems are integrated into a viable, coordinated institution-wide decision support system. Although the term has never been used explicitly, many authors have recognized the need for decision support management. For example, Sprague and Carlson (1982, p. 8) note that one "important dimension of DS is the communication and coordination between decision makers across organizational levels as well as at the same level." And, these authors say (p. 287), "there must be a spectrum of models to serve the decision maker at the strategic, tactical, and operational levels. These models must work together to avoid suboptimization at any one level or in any one functional area."

Norris and Mims (1984, p. 18) state the case for decision support management cogently: "While decision making will remain imperfect, the penalties for poor decision making will be extreme. Under these conditions, it is doubtful that institutions can tolerate the existence of information archipelagos, isolated islands of information and analysis that fail to sustain integrated decision making. Maps and bridges must be built. By bringing together a variety of technologies, analytical perspectives, technical tools, and learnings from research... planning and decision making may be enhanced by creating a true decision support system."

While experts agree on the need for DSM, they do not specifically identify the mechanism by which it can be accomplished. Some authors imply that only highly sophisticated computer and communications technology can implement DSM. Others seem to pin their hopes on the coordination of information through a CIO or information center. Surely, DSM will need both sophisticated technology and reliable information, but I believe that DSM must be participative and that it must emphasize human relations and the needs and perspectives of all parties involved, especially in higher education, where strategic and tactical planning are widely dispersed.

How can information anarchy be prevented, and how can the possibilities of an integrative, participative decision support system be developed? What group is best suited to accomplish these goals? In my opinion, it is not systems analysts, not toolsmiths, not the MIS department, but institutional researchers performing their traditional roles in new and exciting ways.

Traditionally, institutional research has been charged with responsibility for conducting research leading to improved understanding of the possible consequences of alternative decisions affecting an institution or system of postsecondary education. That charge included the collection of relevant data, the making of thoughtful and appropriate analyses, and the interpretation of results to others. Since its responsibilities spanned the institution, its practitioners had to earn the respect and confidence of all participants in the decision-making process.

None of this has changed. But, the method by which these responsibilities will be carried out has. Distributed data bases and micro-led distributed computing inevitably lead to distributed institutional research. The data and methods of analysis are no longer the exclusive domain of IR. Now, they are directly in the hands of the decision makers. Institutional researchers must either learn to perform the roles of DS intermediary, DS facilitator, and, most important, DS manager or resign themselves to answering questionnaires and processing forms.

While some decision makers are already thoroughly familiar with computers and the construction of specific decision support systems, most will welcome the assistance of persons who can help them understand how SDSSs can be modeled and used. IR professionals who have both an understanding of computer modeling and a rapport with decision makers are ideally suited to fill this role of DS intermediary.

A DS facilitator acts as a bridge between the DS technical support people, the toolsmiths, and the needs of decision makers. This role requires persons who are familiar with the details and capabilities of the technology and the uses to which it can and should be put. Most technicians are not familiar with the nature of the academic environment, and most decision makers are not thoroughly conversant with the technology. Informed institutional researchers are adept at both policy and technical matters.

In decision support management, communication and cooperation must be maintained throughout the system. Internal data definitions must be as consistent as possible, and their inconsistencies must be understood and documented. Decisions made in one part of the system must be available as data in other parts. The quality and usefulness of external data bases for specific decision support systems must be judged, as must the usefulness of external DS software packages. Depending on how the management function is interpreted, it can be performed by a CIO or by the staff of an information center. But, decision support management involves a broader perspective than just knowledge about the accessibility and validity of information. It also presumes a thorough understanding of the structure of the institution, its modes of decision making, and the parts that various actors play in the process. It requires persons skilled in interpersonal relations as well as in technology who, respected by all parties, can help the institution's leaders to communicate their vision of what the institution can become. This is a demanding role indeed, but it is one that IR must be prepared to accept.

References

"Can We Turn Down the Heat on the Faculty?" *Technology Review*, 1984, *87* (1), 78.

Execucom Systems Corporation. *University Support Newsletter.* Austin, Texas: Execucom Systems Corporation, September, 1983.

Hample, S. R. "The Impact of Information Technology: Will IR Survive?" Unpublished working paper, Montana State University, Bozeman, February 1983.

Keen, P. G. W., and Scott-Morton, M. S. *Decision Support Systems: An Organizational Perspective.* Reading, Mass.: Addison-Wesley, 1978.

Norris, D. M., and Mims, R. S. "A New Maturity for Institutional Planning and Information Management." *Journal of Higher Education,* 1984, 55 (6).

Plane, D. R. *Quantitative Tools for Decision Support.* Reading, Mass.: Addison-Wesley, forthcoming.

Sprague, R. H., Jr., and Carlson, E. D. *Building Effective Decision Support Systems.* Englewood Cliffs, N.J.: Prentice-Hall, 1982.

Thierauf, R. J. *Decision Support Systems for Effective Planning and Control.* Englewood Cliffs, N.J.: Prentice-Hall, 1982.

Paul Jedamus is head of the Division of Management Science and Information Systems at the University of Colorado–Boulder.

While microcomputers may be easy to acquire and put into use, advance consideration of some pertinent issues will ensure that they are used successfully for planning and management support.

A Jump Ahead...
In Which Direction?

Mark Meredith

As a mother kangaroo reportedly said to her baby, it is no good being one jump ahead if you are headed in the wrong direction. Thus, before you start out in the new direction of microcomputer technology, it is wise to give serious thought to the questions posed in this chapter by a microcomputer enthusiast in a positive spirit. These questions can serve as a checklist for some of the critical issues to be dealt with in administrative and institutional research applications of the new technology. They should help in assessing the impact of this technology on the individual institution and in identifying the multitude of trade-offs that confront the microcomputer user.

What consequences result from a situation where many individual users acquire and use microcomputers instead of a centralized and institutional computer system? On the one hand, microcomputers permit customized use and thus help each user to do his or her job in an individual way. On the other hand, there are problems associated with a variety of individualized and highly personal applications. The considerable range of human differences will significantly affect the implementation of microcomputer technology on the individual campus. A wide range of perspectives and predispositions can generate significant problems. Establishing consensus, meeting everyone's needs, allowing for varied levels of training, and achieving group cohesion in sharing the benefits of using microcomputers will not be an easy task. But, diversity can also produce new ideas and alternative solutions and interpretations, and it can help to generate a more considered end result in planning and management support.

How can staff members be motivated to use and accept microcomputers? Some persons may be eager and willing to use microcomputers, while others may be timid or uncertain about appropriate uses. Demonstrating enthusiasm for this technology at the leadership level will help. Providing assistance for training and for continued use of microcomputers is vital for motivation and acceptance, which will not happen automatically.

Has the user-friendly nature of the technology been oversold? Individuals may be overoptimistic or oversold on the ease and speed with which microcomputers can or should be selected and installed. Consequently, they may fail to recognize many of the potential limitations that need to be addressed. Problems result from such things as making a microcomputer purchase without sufficient investigation or needs assessment, failure to define the anticipated benefits clearly, lack of coordination among users, inadequate technical or analytical expertise among staff, and failure to estimate total resource requirements.

What are the expectations of prospective users? Polling members of the group on this question in both the early and late stages of microcomputer acquisition and implementation is important. A main objective might be to connect the information archipelago of office automation, telecommunications, and data processing (McKenney and McFarlan, 1982).

To what extent are the characteristics of decision makers and users interdependent with the characteristics of the microcomputer system? Such characteristics as organizational structure, communication methods, leadership style, cognitive style, group dynamics, attitudes, expectations, and performance are all important factors in the outcome. Are the right participants assembled into a cohesive, working group for the purpose of planning and implementing a microcomputer system? When planning and implementing a microcomputer system at an institution, administrators typically involve a diverse but representative group of users, managers, and advisers; vendor representatives may also be involved. The group can function formally or informally, and task emphasis can change with each phase of development. It may be necessary for each division and department that will be a major user to be represented, including data processing, purchasing, and administrative areas that have had prior experience with microcomputers. As Lasden (1982) suggests, it is advantageous to involve people who have general management sense in addition to technical skills in attempts to solve technical problems.

Who monitors task group behavior before, during, and after implementation of a microcomputer system? The monitoring of group behavior is essential in order to avoid fragmentation of effort and results. Failure to do so may lead to confusion, redundancy, or omission.

Is there a specific, limited use design for each microcomputer hardware and software product that the buyer should understand in order to maximize the utility of resource commitments and expenditures? Microcomputer products tend to aim for a specific market. Thus, hardware and software designs, despite outward appearances of similarity, may differ significantly due to marketing, engineering, and programming assumptions and oversights. Since the microcomputers that an institution buys are likely to be in use for a number of years, the guiding principle should be caveat emptor. Try to test as many hardware and software products as you can before committing your resources. If an off-the-shelf item imposes limitations on your needs or preferences, perhaps it should be put back on the shelf.

How is one to establish in advance sufficient information and procedural protocols for data input, storage, access, and maintenance to facilitate interchange and shared use of information and software? Users of shared data should fully understand the nature and limitations of data bases to use and interpret them properly. Providing information to support the planning and management effort is the main purpose for using a microcomputer in institutional research. Matters such as how good, appropriate, well defined, created, and interpreted the data are should receive high priority. Proper care and handling of data should be sustained by individual users working independently as well as by microcomputer system users who share data via a network. Many of the methods and understandings of proper use of information that have typically been part of the modus operandi of institutional research will need to be acquired by all users of the system.

How does one deal with erroneous, noncomparable, or inapplicable data? First, one must determine whether data are noncomparable, inapplicable, or erroneous. These things are not always easy to detect in completed reports, and such determination typically requires examination by knowledgeable persons. The possibility of information anarchy that Jedamus describes in Chapter Seven may arise and should be avoided. The need for an institutional information intermediary and the question of who this should be has been argued by Sheehan (1983). Perhaps the best means for identifying and resolving these problems is through the creators and users. Assigning responsibility would seem to be an important step in minimizing the problem.

Are microcomputer-generated and -reported data perceived as more authentic, precise, or accurate by those awed by the technology? This question applies to all data presentations, not just to microcomputer-generated ones. Yet, when users of microcomputer systems in your institution produce reports, does the resulting information take on greater significance because of its source? Users and decision makers should be cautioned against emphasizing information over good judgment. Information should be used as a tool to assist the decision process.

Are you planning to use or already using the right technical tools in terms of microcomputer system capacity, quantity, speed, software, user-friendliness, network configuration, and future modifications? It is essential first to identify clearly the administrative and institutional research files and report systems that you want to incorporate into microcomputer applications. Do you want to do the same things faster, or do you want to do things differently, perhaps with more detailed or with more summary reporting? Do you want more reporting directly from the offices where source data originate? Do you want to expand the file size, do more multiyear trend analysis, or improve administrative communications? Whatever your objectives, including possible new or expanded applications in the future, they should be determined before you talk to microcomputer vendors. It may be appropriate to review analytical expertise in each user office to help determine whether stated microcomputer needs and uses are complete and stable.

Do conflicts exist between traditional data processing personnel and microcomputer system users, and, if they do, can they be resolved? Conflict between data processing staff and microcomputer users throughout an organization can occur in one or more ways. Distributed microcomputer systems may threaten the traditional role and operational data control of the data processing department. Or, the data processing department may continue to regulate or control hardware, software, or procedures for the newer microcomputer systems by imposing restrictions. Such conflicts need to be resolved as soon as possible. Whether they can be resolved and how are questions that deserve attention, but they must be answered within the specific institutional environment.

If a microcomputer network develops, is a centralized information systems office needed to coordinate and oversee it? The answer to this question depends on such things as the existence and effectiveness of a microcomputer user group; the diversity of users' needs; the extent of technical assistance; the size of any network; group dynamics; the locus of data files; the establishment of information and procedural protocols, analysis, and reporting methods; and the probability of network expansion. The need and the ability to share information are perhaps the two most important features of and reasons for a network (Bonner, 1983). The less complex the network is in terms of size, user needs, and number of shared data files, the less need there is for centralized coordination. If a centralized system office is involved, great care should be taken to minimize restrictive controls.

Do total resource requirements for microcomputer systems tend to be greater than estimated? Has every type of cost been accounted for, including direct, indirect, training, and contingency costs? How can microcomputer benefits be estimated for comparison with costs? Direct, initial costs of hardware and software may easily be perceived as those necessary to acquire and implement a microcomputer system. However, total activity and resources connected with the entire system—acquiring it, learning about it, using it, and modifying it—should be explored. It may be useful to talk with colleagues at other institutions who have been through the process to identify total cost and activity, both direct and indirect. Expected benefits and total resources can then be compared, evaluated, and monitored after implementation. Staff time consumed in training, in developing new applications and converting old ones, and in creating additional data to meet increased management support demands are just a few of the ways in which resources can be consumed through the use of microcomputers.

References

Bonner, P. "Networking: What's in It for You." *Personal Computing,* 1983, *7* (10), 128–137.

Lasden, M. "Computer-Aided Decision Making." *Computer Decisions,* 1982, *14* (11), 156–172.

McKenney, J. L., and McFarlan, F. W. "The Information Archipelago: Maps and Bridges." *Harvard Business Review,* 1982, *60* (5), 109–119.

Sheehan, B. S. *Measurement for Decision Support.* Calgary: Faculty of Management, University of Calgary, 1983.

Staman, E. M. "Computing and Office Automation—Changing Variables." In *The AIR Professional File,* no. 10. Tallahassee, Fla.: Association for Institutional Research, 1981.

Mark Meredith is director of management information exchange and analysis and a member of the graduate faculty at the University of Colorado–Boulder. His twenty years of experience in both public and private higher education include institutional research, information systems development and testing, long-range campus planning, support of budget planning and policy formulation, and teaching.

Microcomputer technology is direct, personal, and especially well suited for the task of decision support. Perhaps the only thing that exceeds its usefulness is the expectation of a new or potential user.

Conclusion: Using Microcomputers for Planning and Management Support

William L. Tetlow

In *The Micro Millenium*, Christopher Evans (1979, p. 5) convincingly asserts that a transformation of world society is taking place at all levels and that the "computer revolution" will affect "every being on earth in every aspect of his or her life." What higher education administrators and managers are experiencing is not therefore a unique phenomenon but rather part of what Toffler (1981, p. 4) called "colliding waves of change." Microcomputer technology is being acquired and used in a very eclectic fashion for personal, professional, and business reasons. Because the technology is so new, the equipment choices abundant, the technical terms unfamiliar, and the advice contradictory and misleading, there is a clear need for a comprehensive overview of the potential uses of the technology. This sourcebook was conceived to meet the portion of that need that pertains to the use of microcomputers for higher education planning and management support.

As Leah Hutten notes in Chapter Four, the institutional research and planning office has taken a lead in introducing new technology to higher education. Thus, it is appropriate for expert discussions of that topic to be found in this *New Directions* series. In Chapter Six, Vinod Chachra notes that the potential impact is awesome as both computer and communications technology combine. He suggests that one useful way of measuring the impact of a new technology is to estimate by what factor it has multiplied human capabilities to do a given task. Since both communications and computer technology are million multipliers, the effect of the two combined is a million times a million. Thus, he states that the advances we are seeing today do not begin to represent the possibilities that are sure to exist in the future.

What has caused the extremely rapid infusion of microcomputer technology into our higher education environment? The answers are many, but analysts have cited a huge pent-up demand among educators for control over the computing environment so that they could make it more responsive and personally useful in their professional lives. Hutten states that by the late 1970s access to large computers had become so restricted that they were often inaccessible and unable to meet some user needs and that large systems were not fulfilling the needs that they had helped to create. Chachra proposes that the very purpose of personal computing is to permit the user to create his or her own personalized environment.

J. Lloyd Suttle argues in Chapter Three that the ability to gather, store, retrieve, analyze, integrate, and disseminate data is at the core of the institutional research function. But, of even greater importance is the ability to translate this information into a form that can and will be used for management decision making and planning. All the authors assert that microcomputers are especially useful in this regard. Paul L. Brinkman reminds us in Chapter Two that data become informative if and when they reduce someone's uncertainty but that this process does not happen automatically or even easily and that microcomputers significantly reduce the effort involved.

According to Brinkman, there has been a widespread feeling among senior managers that the typical management information system (MIS) has not been very helpful because it ignores their particular needs. The microcomputer was the first truly personal computing device, and it enabled novices to portray data and information graphically. Suttle, Hutten, and Brinkman all applaud these features of microcomputers. Brinkman cites research indicating that graphic presentations enhance the rate and quantity of information transfer. A typical result is that the individuals find that certain types of analysis become easier and that some forms of graphic presentation media, including spreadsheets, are more likely to lead to insight. As Brinkman notes, it is hard to overemphasize the difference between a desktop device that can become an extension of one's self akin to an artist's palette and brush and a device under someone else's direction that supplies management reports, however informative and necessary those reports may be.

Chachra's experience indicates that personal computer users very soon begin to interact with other personal computer users, exchanging products or working together on the same activity. Once again, the communications aspect of this technology is intertwined significantly with the computational activities. Suttle contends that the ability to communicate effectively rests at the core of the institutional research function and that electronic mail, electronic computer conferencing, data exchange, and so forth are increasingly being used by institutional researchers. In Chapter Five, Derek M. Jamieson and Kenneth H. MacKay provide a useful exposition of the problems and potential of electronic communications from firsthand experience, and their analysis is replicated by both Suttle and Hutten, although all contend that institutional researchers have barely scratched the surface of this new technology. Jamieson and MacKay note, however, that communicating is an especially human endeavor and that people resist change. They suggest that new metaphors are needed to describe the new potential accurately so that we do not impede the acceptance of new forms of communicating. Their comparison with a previous generation's use of the terms *wireless* and *horseless carriage* very effectively makes their point. Those who have experimented with electronic computer conferencing know precisely what these gentlemen are suggesting, because it is a form of communication that has no predecessor. On the one hand, problems of distance, time, scheduling, facilities, and irrelevant discourses that waste time are obliterated. On the other hand, humor, intonation, nuances of expression conveyed through body language, and other aids to human communication are likewise obliterated. It is a strange feeling to understand that a joke was intended when you encounter the printed assurance of a "ha-ha" inserted to offset potential misunderstandings.

The purpose of communication in our context is the support that it can lend to the decision-making process. Jamieson and MacKay, Brinkman, and Jedamus in Chapter Seven focus on the emergence of decision support systems as the natural evolutionary successor to management information systems. Brinkman says that the strategy that seems to be taking hold features an interactive approach, in which the decision aid assists the decision maker to clarify assumptions and preferences and to achieve greater control over the various components of the process. Jamieson and MacKay consider decision support systems as a class of computerized aids that offer personalized facilities to help an executive make decisions.

Brinkman reminds us, however, that no matter how sophisticated the media and the models for decision support become, managers will continue to require access to data and information. In Chapter Eight, Meredith asks two questions of concern to several authors: How do you establish in advance sufficient information and procedural protocols for data input, storage, access, and maintenance that will facilitate interchange and shared use of information and software? and What consequences result from a situation where a diversity of individual users acquires and uses microcomputers instead of a centralized computer system?

Jedamus is concerned about the possibility in which separate decision centers possessing ample computing facilities and unarticulated bits and pieces of data produce a condition of information anarchy. His solution is decision support management, a role that, he contends, is perfectly suited to the veteran institutional researcher. The institutional research professional can prevent the proliferation of information archipelagos—those isolated islands of information and analysis that, claim Norris and Simms (1984), fail to sustain integrated decision making.

Jamieson and MacKay assert that networks are going to play an increasingly important role in institutional research. Local area networks and campuswide and national networks are seen as becoming essential for planning activities. Chachra tackles this subject as well and provides guidance on the proper integration of micros, minis, and mainframes. As Suttle expresses it, through telecommunications, microcomputers can be used to gain access to the processing power of other computers, to the people who use those systems, and to the information stored in them.

That microcomputers are important, even essential, components of higher education management is a premise shared by all the authors. The decision to purchase a microcomputer, however, is a difficult one, because there are literally hundreds of hardware models and thousands of software programs from which to choose. As Suttle puts it, advances in microcomputer marketing seem to exceed the advances in microcomputer technology.

In Chapter Four, Hutten demystifies the jargon of this "high-tech" jungle of microcomputing and explains the essentials of hardware and software. Both she and Suttle offer concrete suggestions for microcomputer purchase and use, and Chachra provides guidance on role separation and delineation for all three principal players in the game of computing on campus.

Suttle advises readers not to wait until they think they know fully and precisely how they are going to use a microcomputer before investing in one. Chachra estimates the useful life of equipment to be not more than five years; four years are reasonable, and three are "most likely." Jamieson and MacKay assert that the selection problem may be eased somewhat once one recognizes that the selection of one of the three major generic operating systems is essential, because all applications software is technically associated with an operating system. According to Suttle, the day you take your new microcomputer out of the box is the day you start planning your next system.

Several authors warn that full costs are often overlooked in the haste to acquire and use microcomputers. Supplies, maintenance, insurance, security devices, power regulators, connecting cables—the list is long—all add significantly to the total cost. Even more significant, however, is the fact that hardware costs are considerably less important than software and personnel costs. By 1990, says Chachra, approximately 10 percent of the total cost of computing will be attributed to hardware and approximately 90 percent to software and personnel. Therefore, he advises, a personnel impact statement is a necessary piece of information in this particular decision-making problem. Both

Mark Meredith and others warn of the cost of training, which is essential if microcomputers are to contribute to more effective decision making.

As I noted in Chapter One, the transformation to a new societal norm does not happen instantaneously, and many managers in higher education are still mired in the first stage of the technological development involving microcomputers. To achieve the third stage, in which new directions or uses are discovered that grow out of the technology itself, is a goal to which I believe all the authors subscribe. Higher education cannot continue doing business as usual when the world is awash in colliding waves of societal change. Acquiring this technology and putting it to productive use are essential to the efficacy of higher education.

I think that Suttle expresses the conviction of us all—perhaps the only thing about microcomputers that exceeds their usefulness in institutional research and planning is the expectation of new or potential users. I hope that this sourcebook will enable readers to acquire a basic understanding of the uses and abuses of microcomputer technology and, as a result, realistic expectations.

References

Norris, D. M., and Mims, R. S. "A New Maturity for Institutional Planning and Information Management." *The Journal of Higher Education,* 1984, *55* (6), forthcoming.
Evans, C. *The Micro Millenium.* London: Viking, 1979.
Toffler, A. *The Third Wave.* New York: Bantam, 1981.

William L. Tetlow is director of the Management Products Division at the National Center for Higher Education Management Systems in Boulder, Colorado.

Index

A

ADABAS, 67
American Statistical Association, 49
Anthony, R., 12, 24
APL, 56
Apple microcomputer, 3, 9-10
Artificial intelligence (AI): concept and development of, 19-21; and microcomputers, 23
Assembler, 48
Association for Institutional Research (AIR), 9

B

Backups, concept of, 42
BASIC, 35, 48, 56
Baud, concept of, 46
Bell Labs, 61
BITNET, 27
Bits, concept of, 41
Blin, J. M., 21, 24
Bloom, A. M., 34, 38
Bloomfield, S. D., 16, 24
Bonner, P., 23, 24, 90, 91
Brinkman, P. T., 2, 11-25, 94, 95
Bubble memory, features of, 43

C

C language, 48
Carlson, E. D., 14, 16, 25, 79, 80, 83, 85
Cathode ray tube (CRT), 44
Central processing unit (CPU), 41
Chachra, V., 2, 63-75, 94, 96
Change, and computerization, 6-7, 10
Chomsky, N., 20
COBOL, 48
Cognitive psychology, and computer-based information systems, 21-22
Colorado-Boulder, University of, specific decision support systems at, 78
Communication: analysis of microcomputers for, 53-62, 94-95; features for, 50-51; issues in, 61-62

COMPAQ microcomputer, 3
Complementary-metal-oxide-semiconductor (CMOS) memory, 43
Computation, evolution of, 28
Computer-aided design/computer-aided manufacturing (CAD/CAM), 50, 67, 72
Computer-based information systems (CBISs): analysis of, 11-25; background on, 11-12; concepts in, 12-18; and microcomputers, 22-24; summary on, 24; and supportive research, 18-22; trends in, 12
Computerization: analysis of second wave of, 5-10; background on, 5-6; and change, 6-7, 10; conclusion on, 74-75; costs of, 65-66; and decision support management 77-85; micros, minis, and mainframes for, 63-75; multiplier effect of, 64; and societal trends, 7-8, 9-10; and technological development, 8
Computing: charging for, 70-71; decentralization of, 71-74; job shop mode of, 70; library mode of 70-71; types of, 69; utility mode of, 70
Computing center, responsibility of, 71-72
Control program/microcomputers (CP/M), 47, 61
Cornell University, and EFPM, 33

D

Data: concept of, 12-13; shared, issues of, 89
Data base management system (DBMS), concept and development of, 14-15
Data base systems, features for, 50
Data management, applications of, 34-35
Decentralization: managing, 71-74; trend toward, 9
Decision support management (DSM): analysis of, 77-85; background on,

99

DSM *(continued)*
77-78; concept of, 83; and information anarchy, 81-82; and institutional research, 83-84
Decision support systems (DSSs): background on, 78; concept and development of, 17-18, 78; iterative design of, 79; microcomputers for, 56-57, 95-96; right-brained, 21; structure of, in higher education, 78-81
Department, responsibility of, 72-73
Departmental computing, concept of, 69
Departmental workstations, microcomputers for, 59-60
DIALOG, 34
Digital Equipment Corporation, 50
Digital Research Corporation, 61
Digitizer, features of, 44
Disk drive, features of, 42
Display, 44
Double-sided double-density (DS/DD) diskettes, 42
Duda, R. O., 20, 25
Dunn, J., 34

E

EDUCOM, Financial Planning Model (EFPM) of, 32, 33
EDUMAIL, 58
EDUNET, 33, 34
Electronic computer conferencing (ECC): microcomputers for, 58-59; potential of, 8
Electronic data processing (EDP), concept and development of, 13
Electronic disk, features of, 43
Electronic forms, and microcomputers, 59
Electronic message systems (EMSs), microcomputers for, 58
Electronic spreadsheet: applications of, 31-32; features for, 49; and microcomputers, 22-23, 57; potential of, 8
Electronic worksheets, dedicated, 23
ELIZA, 20-21
E-MAIL, 58
ERIC, 29, 34
Evans, C., 1, 3, 6, 10, 93, 97
Execucom Systems Corporation, 1*n*, 79, 84
Expert systems, concept and development of, 20

F

File server, 60
File transfer program, applications of, 34
Firmware, concept of, 42
Floppy disk, features of, 42
FORTRAN, 48, 67
Fridlund, A. J., 10
Fuzzy sets, concept and development of, 21

G

Gabel, D., 16, 25
Garfield, E., 20, 25
Global computing, concept of, 69
Graphics: analytical, 50; applications of, 32-33; and cognitive psychology, 22; features for, 49-50; and mediation, 22
Gray, P. E., 81
Greene, J. O., 23, 25
Grosch, H., 63
Grosch's Law, 63, 74

H

Hackman, J. D., 22, 25
Hample, S. R., 82, 84
Hardware: concept of, 40; costs of, 65; features of, 41-47; for input, 43-44; issues of, 89; for output, 44-47
Harvard University, budget planning models at, 32
Higher Education Data System, 34
Hopkins, D. S. P., 16, 17, 18, 25
Huber, G. P., 22, 25
Hutten, L. R., 2, 39-52, 93, 94, 95, 96

I

IBM, 32, 39, 50, 65; Personal Computer of, 47, 61
Icons, concept of, 48
Idea processors, and microcomputers, 23
IMS, 67
Individuals, responsibilities of, 73-74
Information: anarchy of, 81-82, 89, 96; archipelago of, 83, 88, 96; concept of, 13
Information assistant, 59

Information society, trend toward, 7-8
Information Toxicity Syndrome, 10
Institutional research: analysis of microcomputers for, 27-38; and decision support management, 83-84; defined, 28; evolution of, 28; responsibility of, 83
Integrated voice data (IVD) facilities, 61
Intelligent terminal, 59
Intelligent workstations, microcomputers as 33-34, 58-59
Interactive financial planning simulations (IFPS), 1*n*, 79
International Standards Organization (ISO), 60

J

Jamieson, D. M., 2, 53-62, 95, 96
Jarett, I. M., 22, 25
Jedamus, P., 3, 77-85, 89, 95-96
Jobs, S., 3
Johnson, R. R., 29, 38

K

K, concept of, 41
Kaplan, A., 15, 25
Keen, P. G. W., 19, 22, 25, 78-79, 85
Keyboard, features of, 43-44
Knowledge engineering systems, concept of, 20
Kruglinski, D., 15, 25

L

Languages, programming, 48
Lasden, M., 88, 91
Laser recording, features of, 43
Lawrence, L. L., 25
Liquid crystal display (LCD), features of, 45
LISP, 67
Local area networks (LANs): microcomputers for, 60-61; and personal computing, 69
Local computing, concept of, 69
Lotus Development Corporation, 1*n*
Lotus 1-2-3, 1*n*, 28, 32, 34

M

McCredie, J. W., 36, 38
McFarlan, F. W., 88, 91

MacKay, K. H., 2, 53-62, 95, 96
McKeefery, W. J., 64, 75
McKenney, J. L., 22, 25, 88, 91
Magnetic tapes, features of, 53
MAILNET, 58
Mainframes, application areas for, 66-67
Management control: and decision support systems, 80-81; and information system, 12
Management information system (MIS): concept and development of, 14; and modeling, 17
Management science, concept and development of, 18, 23
Management support, kinds of, 12
Mann, R. L., 28, 29, 38
Massachusetts Institute of Technology (M.I.T.): interactive computing work at, 17; strategic planning at, 81
Massy, W. F., 16, 25
Mediation, and microcomputers, 22
Memory and storage, features of, 41-43
Menus, concept of, 48
Meredith, M., 3, 87-91, 95, 97
Microcomputers: analysis of, for institutional research, 27-38; applications of, 28-35, 68-69; characteristics, 88; compatible, 47; and computer-based information systems, 22-24; conclusions on, 93-97; for distributed information processing, 53-62; example of using, 27-28; expectations about, 88; guidelines for using, 35-38; impact of, 37-38, 87-88; implementing system for, 36-37; increased interest in, 94; information system roles of, 23; as intelligent terminal, 33-34, 58-59; issues related to, 87-91; portable, 46-47; purchasing, 35-36, 40, 51-52, 96; resource requirements for, 90-91; security of, 31; technical tools for, 89-90; typical system configuration for, 46
Microprocessor, features of, 41
Microsoft Corporation, 61
Microsoft disc-operating system (MS-DOS), 47, 61
Microware: analysis of, 39-52; background on, 39-40; hard, 41-47; soft, 47-51
Mims, R. S., 78, 83, 85, 96, 97
Minicomputers, application areas for, 67-68

Modeling: concept and development of, 15–17; and microcomputers, 23
Modem, features of, 46
Monitor, features of, 44–45
Montgomery, J. R., 34, 38
Mouse, features of, 44
MPSX, 67
Multicriteria decision making (MCDM): concept and development of, 19; and fuzzy sets, 21

N

Naisbitt, J., 2, 3, 7, 8, 9, 10
Natural language (NL) processing: concept and development of, 20–21; and microcomputers, 23
Negoita, C. V., 21, 25
Networking: concept of, 43; features of, 90; local area, 60–61, 69; role of, 96; trend toward, 9
Norris, D. M., 32, 38, 78, 83, 85, 96, 97
Numerical analysis, applications of, 30–32

O

Operating system: for communication, 61; features of, 47–48
Operational control: and decision support systems, 80–81; and information system, 12
Operations research and management science (OR/MS): concept and development of, 18; and microcomputers, 23
Optimization models, concept of, 16

P

Participatory democracy, trend toward, 9
Pascal, 48
Personal computers. *See* Microcomputers
Personal computing, concept of, 69
Personnel: conflicts between, 90; costs of, 66
Pixels, 44–45
Plane, D. R., 78, 85
Plotter, features of, 46
Printer, features of, 45–46
Programming: custom, 35; languages, 48

R

Random access memory (RAM), features of, 41–42, 43, 49
Raster scan, 44–45
Read-only memory (ROM), features of, 41, 42, 48
Ridge, J. W., 33, 38
Rivett, P., 18, 25
Robey, D., 22, 25

S

Saunders, L. E., 34, 38
Saupe, J. L., 28, 38
Schmid, C., 22, 25
Schmid, S., 22, 25
Schroeder, R. G., 18, 25
Scott-Morton, M. S., 78–79, 85
Screen, use of, 44
Self-help, trend toward, 9–10
Sheehan, B. S., 89, 91
Shortliffe, E. H., 20, 25
Simon, H. A., 17, 19, 25
Simulation models, concept of, 16
Single-sided single-density (SS/SD) diskettes, 42
Smart desk, 59
SNOBOL, 67
Software: and applications programs, 48–51; concept of, 40; costs of, 65–66; features of, 47–51; issues of, 89
Solomon, M. B., 63, 75
Sonenstein, B., 25
Sorcim, Inc., 1*n*
Source, The, 34
Specific decision support systems (SDSSs), potential of, 78, 80, 81, 82
Sprague, R. H., Jr., 14, 16, 25, 79, 80, 83, 85
Staman, E. M., 91
State University of New York at Albany, custom program at, 35
Statistical analysis packages: applications of, 30–31; features for, 49
Statistical Package for the Social Sciences (SPSS), 32
Stewart, T. R., 5, 10
Strategic planning: and decision support systems, 80–81; and information system, 12
Sumeria, data processing in, 13
SuperCalc, 1*n*, 32

Suttle, J. L., 2, 27-38, 94, 95, 96, 97
System, concept of, 13

T

Tactical planning, and decision support systems, 80-81
Technological development, stages of, 8
Telecommunications, applications of, 33-34
TELENET, 28, 33
Telephones, private or computerized branch exchanges for, 61-62
Terminal, use of, 44
Terminal emulation program, applications of, 33
Tetlow, W. L., 1-10, 93-97
Thierauf, R. J., 79, 85
Timm, N. H., 17, 25
Toffler, A., 1, 3, 6, 7, 10, 93, 97
Tracks, concept of, 42
Trends, societal, and computerization, 7-8, 9-10
Tschectelin, J. D., 25
Tufts University, and data exchange, 34

U

United Kingdom, operations research in, 18
U.S. Department of Commerce, 7

UNIX, 47, 61
Updegrove, D. A., 16, 24

V

Very large-scale integration (VLSI), 41 68
Virginia Polytechnic Institute and State University, device-to-port ratio at, 68
Voice mail, and telephones, 62

W

Western Electric, 61
Winchester disk, features of, 42-43
Wizenbaum's work, 20-21
Word processing: applications of, 29-30; features for, 48-49; microcomputers for, 54-56; training for, 54-55

Y

Yager, R. R., 21, 25
Yale University, budget planning models at, 32
Young, L. F., 21, 25

Z

Zeleny, M., 14, 18, 21, 25
Zinsser, M., 30, 38

Ministry of Education & Training
MET Library
13th Floor, Mowat Block, Queen's Park
Toronto   M7A 1L2

U.S. POSTAL SERVICE
STATEMENT OF OWNERSHIP, MANAGEMENT AND CIRCULATION
(Required by 39 U.S.C. 3685)

1. TITLE OF PUBLICATION	A. PUBLICATION NO.	2. DATE OF FILING
New Directions for Institutional Research	0 9 8 8 3 0	9/30/84

3. FREQUENCY OF ISSUE	A. NO. OF ISSUES PUBLISHED ANNUALLY	B. ANNUAL SUBSCRIPTION PRICE
quarterly	4	$35 inst/$25 indv

4. COMPLETE MAILING ADDRESS OF KNOWN OFFICE OF PUBLICATION *(Street, City, County, State and ZIP Code) (Not printers)*
433 California St., San Francisco (SF County), CA 94104

5. COMPLETE MAILING ADDRESS OF THE HEADQUARTERS OR GENERAL BUSINESS OFFICES OF THE PUBLISHERS *(Not printers)*
433 California St., San Francisco (SF County), CA 94104

6. FULL NAMES AND COMPLETE MAILING ADDRESS OF PUBLISHER, EDITOR, AND MANAGING EDITOR *(This item MUST NOT be blank)*

PUBLISHER *(Name and Complete Mailing Address)*
Jossey-Bass Inc., Publishers, 433 California St., S.F., CA 94104

EDITOR *(Name and Complete Mailing Address)*
Patrick Terenzini, Admin. Bldg. 260, SUNY at Albany, Albany, NY 12222

MANAGING EDITOR *(Name and Complete Mailing Address)*
Allen Jossey-Bass, 433 California St., San Francisco, CA 94104

7. OWNER *(If owned by a corporation, its name and address must be stated and also immediately thereunder the names and addresses of stockholders owning or holding 1 percent or more of total amount of stock. If not owned by a corporation, the names and addresses of the individual owners must be given. If owned by a partnership or other unincorporated firm, its name and address, as well as that of each individual must be given. If the publication is published by a nonprofit organization, its name and address must be stated.) (Item must be completed.)*

FULL NAME	COMPLETE MAILING ADDRESS
Jossey-Bass Inc., Publishers	433 California St., S.F., CA 94104

For names and addresses of stockholders, see attached list.

8. KNOWN BONDHOLDERS, MORTGAGEES, AND OTHER SECURITY HOLDERS OWNING OR HOLDING 1 PERCENT OR MORE OF TOTAL AMOUNT OF BONDS, MORTGAGES OR OTHER SECURITIES *(If there are none, so state)*

FULL NAME	COMPLETE MAILING ADDRESS
Same as #7	

9. FOR COMPLETION BY NONPROFIT ORGANIZATIONS AUTHORIZED TO MAIL AT SPECIAL RATES *(Section 411.3, DMM only)*
The purpose, function, and nonprofit status of this organization and the exempt status for Federal income tax purposes *(Check one)*

☐ (1) HAS NOT CHANGED DURING PRECEDING 12 MONTHS
☐ (2) HAS CHANGED DURING PRECEDING 12 MONTHS
(If changed, publisher must submit explanation of change with this statement.)

10. EXTENT AND NATURE OF CIRCULATION	AVERAGE NO. COPIES EACH ISSUE DURING PRECEDING 12 MONTHS	ACTUAL NO. COPIES OF SINGLE ISSUE PUBLISHED NEAREST TO FILING DATE
A. TOTAL NO. COPIES *(Net Press Run)*	1969	1989
B. PAID CIRCULATION		
1. Sales through dealers and carriers, street vendors and counter sales	325	15
2. Mail Subscription	975	974
C. TOTAL PAID CIRCULATION *(Sum of 10B1 and 10B2)*	1300	989
D. FREE DISTRIBUTION BY MAIL, CARRIER OR OTHER MEANS SAMPLES, COMPLIMENTARY, AND OTHER FREE COPIES	139	111
E. TOTAL DISTRIBUTION *(Sum of C and D)*	1439	1100
F. COPIES NOT DISTRIBUTED		
1. Office use, left over, unaccounted, spoiled after printing	530	889
2. Return from news agents	0	0
G. TOTAL *(Sum of E, F1 and 2 — should equal net press run shown in A)*	1969	1989

11. I certify that the statements made by me above are correct and complete

SIGNATURE AND TITLE OF EDITOR, PUBLISHER, BUSINESS MANAGER, OR OWNER
John R. Ward   Vice-President

PS Form 3526, July 1981